THE BIBLICAL BEGINNING AND ENDING OF TITHES

A Revelation of Truth for Modern Day Christians

By

Reverend Eugene McKinley Wilson, Sr

A HISTORICAL RESEARCH EXPOSE'

ISBN: 0-7596-8759-5 (e-book)
ISBN: 0-7596-8760-9 (Paperback)

1stBooks - rev. 08/16/02

FORWARD

My research of the Old Testament states that according to the requirement of the Mosaic Law, one tithe was donated once a year for the purpose of completely supplying the Levites for the upkeep of the tabernacle, for their needs, their cares and their wants. The third year tithes were collected for the Israelite widows and the orphans.

Tithing, however, is not a New Testament requirement. Jesus Christ fulfilled the Mosaic law and the prophets. Therefore, the New Testament Church is to be financed by free - will offerings. Every Christian must give under the direction of the Holy Spirit. Spiritual gifts differ in the body of Christ, but all Christians have the Spiritual Gift of giving freely for the cause of Christ.

My extensive sermon on the theme: 'THE BIBLICAL BEGINNING AND ENDING OF TITHES" has been exhaustively presented to you by my research of bibles, history and theology. I have humbly written what the Lord Jesus Christ has moved me to write for His glory and honor and the betterment of the Christian Church.

Reverend Eugene M. Wilson, Sr.

ACKNOWLEDGMENTS

I must express my greatest and most profound appreciation to everyone who has made a contribution to me in my efforts to read the Bibles, the commentaries, the dictionaries, the histories, the philosophy, and the theology books that I have read in my research and compilation of the material that I have gathered to write the Sermon "THE BIBLICAL BEGINNING AND ENDING OF TITHES."

The research for a sermon differs from any other kind of research, because it is difficult to find a partner for sermon research. But I found an extraordinary research partner and an excellent editor in a Mr. John J. Williams, a most outstanding fellow who has devoted his entire life to teaching and counseling people. If John J. Williams were to have been a lover of money, he could have been a multi-millionaire several years in the arrear.

I find that I am expressless when I think of the great sacrifices that my adorable wife has made; while I have been researching, studying and writing the sermon on "BIBLICAL TITHING."

I also wish to express my thanks to Mr. Johnson, the manager of AU Bey Office Service for his expert computer Service. Thanks to a Mr. Henri Forget of Weirsdale, Fl., for his expert editorial service. Thanks to Dean Gene Rice of Howard University School of Divinity for his most outstanding critique and direction in advising in the selection of material for the Sermon. And I shall ever be grateful and indebted to Reverend Dr. Floyd M. Shealy, Ed.D., President of American

Christian College and Seminary of Oklahoma City, Oklahoma for his examining the text and his encouraging letter on my sermon, "THE BIBLICAL BEGINNING AND ENDING OF TITHES."

Reverend Eugene McKinley Wilson, Sr.

INTRODUCTION

Please allow me to explain from the outset that this research revelation is not intended to condemn or indict all Christian ministers of improper tithing practices. However, it is my primary objective to reveal the truth about "biblical tithes". I firmly believe that the conduct of a God-called minister must be influenced by the Lord. The preacher's religious actions and business practices must be biblically sound. With spiritual proof, Christians of today will be able to discern biblical truth from hidden intents of the heart.

The research document will give spiritual proof that the New Testament Christians are not required to pay tithes. You will clearly see for yourself that the Lord was not speaking to the Gentile Christians in Malachi 3:10, when He said:

"Bring all tithes in the storehouse, that there may be meat in mine house, and prove me now herewith, said the lord of host, if I will not open for you the windows of heaven and pour out for you a blessing that there shall not be room enough to receive it."

Reverend Eugene M. Wilson, Sr.

Leviticus and the Beginning of Tithes

My study and research for Leviticus begins with the greatest contributor of the Old Testament, Abram, whose name was changed to Abraham.

Abraham, the son of Terah, oldest brother of Nahor and Haran, was born in Ur of the Chaldees. Chaldees was an ancient though modern country when this historic event was written. There was ever-running water and libraries during this time.

Abram Called by the Lord

Abraham remained in Ur of the Chaldees of Haran until he was seventy-five years of age. One day the Lord spoke to Abraham and said, "Get thee out of thy country, and from their kindred, and from thy father's house, unto a land that I will show thee, and I will make thy name great, and thou shall be a blessing and I will bless them that bless thee, and I will curse him that curseth the, and in thee shall all families of the earth be blessed (Genesis 12:1-3).

Without hesitation or procrastination with his family, Abraham left Ur of the Chaldees. He did not know where he was going, but Abraham obeyed the voice of the Lord.

It seemed rather odd to Abraham, who lived in a country where the people had a polytheistic religion, but Abraham recognized the voice of the lord.

The progression of Abraham's journey is as follows:

When Abraham left Ur, he went to Sumer, Aleppo, Palma, Amurr, Damascus, Shechem, Zoan, and Beeersheba. Abraham was looking for a city whose builder and maker was God. Abraham had developed the spirit of desire of the nearness of God.

The stories of the patriarchs, Abraham, Isaac and Jacob, occupy most of the book of Genesis. First, there is God's call to his constant guidance of Abraham. Abraham's departure for a new land is spiritually motivated. God thrust him out from his kindred and father's house into a new existence. His life in a new land is designed to lead to a great destiny. The forming of a new nation, which will be a blessing to the whole earth. Abraham's calling is seen as God's rejection of polytheism or worship of many gods. Abraham's wholehearted response to God is stressed.

Abraham departed from Haran, as the lord told him. He erected a string of alters in a new land, then he heard the voice of the Lord and Worshipped Him (Genesis 12:7,8,13, 13:4,18). Abraham believed God's promise that he would have a son, Abraham's obedience to God caused god to make the covenant of circumcision with Abraham. God's purpose was to redeem all mankind through Abraham.

Abraham adopted his wife, Sarai, as his sister at Haran in Upper Mesopotamia because the law allows a man to adopt his wife as his sister regardless of the actual blood ties. The act of adopting a man's wife as his sister give her special standing in the society. This act of adopting explained why Abraham presented Sarai as his sister (Genesis 12:9-20).

Moses Appointed Devine Leader

Abraham fathered a son at an old age and his wife, Sarai, named the boy Isaac. Isaac fathered two sons, Esau and Jacob. Jacob fathered twelve sons. Moses became the son of Nun, a descendent of Jacob. Moses is the greatest writer of the Old Testament and is the author of Leviticus, the book of the Old Testament.

Abraham Becomes the First Tither

"After returned from defeating Chedorlaomer and kings allied with him, the king of Sodom came out to meet him in the valley. Shaveh, that is the kings' valley. Then Melchizedek, king of Salem, brought bread and wine. He blessed Abram saying blessed be Abram by god most high, creator of heaven and earth high; who delivered your enemies unto your hands. Then Abram give a tenth of everything" (Genesis 14:17-20). Jacob vowed to give a tenth of his gains to God (Genesis 28:20-22).

Sacred Basic Offering in Leviticus

The biblical outline is as follows:

1. The alter sacrifices
2. The consecration and conduct of priesthood
3. The enactment respecting the purification of uncleanness
4. The kind of animals used for sacrifices
5. The sacrifices of meat on the day of atonement
6. Ordained to propitiate for all omission and faultiness in sacrifices during the year
7. The purity of the priesthood

Note: Time does not allow me to expand on each of these basic offerings.

Moses Wrote Leviticus

Moses wrote the Leviticus shortly after the Lord had written the Ten Commandments and before Moses left Mt. Sania. God called Moses into the tent and commanded him to write Leviticus. Moses wrote as they fell from the mouth of God. It took one month to complete the writing of Leviticus.

Leviticus is called the book of holiness. That is what a holy god required of His people. Leviticus is devoted to the worship of the redeemed people of God. God has redeemed the people of Israel from slavery in Egypt. Now God was carrying Israel through a cleansing process. The offering is an act of God's mercy to an unlimited extent.

Explanation of the Basic Offerings

The basic offerings listed in Leviticus are:

1. The burnt offering was to make payment for sin in general. It showed a person's devotion to God.
2. The meat or grain offering was to show honor and respect to God in worship. It acknowledged that all we have belongs to God.
3. The peace or fellowship offering was to express gratitude to God. It symbolized peace and fellowship with God.
4. The sin offering was to make payment for unintentional sins of uncleanness, neglect or thoughtlessness. It restored the sinner to fellowship with God. It also showed the seriousness of sin.
5. The trespass of guilt offering was to make payment for sin against God and others. A sacrifice was made to God and the injured person was repaired or compensated. Christ, the perfect offering, replaced all the offerings because Christ's death and His resurrection take away the consequences of sin.

Moses Wrote Other Laws for Israel

After the law of the offerings had been given, the Lord give Moses the Law of Consecration of Aaron and his sons the law of Leviticus and the priest art the first law given because the office of the priest was the most important office. In chapter 17, Moses is instructed to tell Aaron, his son and the children of Israel where the acceptable place of sacrifice is to be located.

Chapter 18 covers the law regulating the personal relationship of the redeemed people: "And the Lord spoke unto Moses saying, speak unto the congregation of the children of Israel and say unto them, I am the Lord you God."

Chapter 20, the Lord spoke unto Moses saying: "Sanctify yourselves therefore and be ye holy for I am the Lord your God. And ye shall keep my statues and do them: I am the Lord who sanctifieth you, and the man who committeth adultery with another man's wife, even he who committeth adultery with his neighbor's wife, the adulterer and adulteress shall surely be put to death. If a man lie with mankind, as he lieth with a woman, both of them have committed an abomination; they shall surely be put to death, their blood shall be put to death, their blood shall be upon them."

Chapter 21 covers the feast of the Lord: "And the Lord spoke unto Moses, and saying speak unto the children of Israel and say unto them concerning the feast of the Lord which ye shall proclaim to be holy convocations, even these are my feasts."

Chapter 24 covers the kind of oil and lighting to be used in the tabernacle: The shewbread and punishment for blasphemy.

Chapter 26 cover the continuation of the law of the land: "Yes shall make no idols nor carved images, neither near you up a standing image, neither shall ye set up any images of stone in your land to bow down unto it, for I am the Lord your God. Ye shall keep my Sabbath and reverence in my sanctuary; I am the Lord. If ye walk in my statues and keep my commandments and do them; then I will give you rain in due season and the land shall yield her increase and the trees of the fields shall yield their fruit."

The Lord Warns of Israel Disobedience

The Lord gives the Israelites a warning of six ways he could chastise them for violating his statues:

1. Distress
2. Drought
3. Beasts
4. Disease
5. Famine
6. Dispersion (Leviticus 26:16-39)

But the Abrahamic covenant remains despite the disobedience of the Jews and Israelites.

Chapter 27 cover dedicated persons. "And the Lord spoke unto the children of Israel and He said unto them: when a man shall make a special vow, the person shall be for the Lord by thy valuation. And the valuation shall be of the male from twenty years old, even unto sixty years old, even thy valuation shall be shekels." (Leviticus 27:1-13). The verses 1-13 describes the amount of silver shekels a person must pay when one makes a special vow. Verses 14-25 describes the requirements for a man to sanctify his house. A man was also required to sanctify his field and was required to pay fifty shekels of silver. In verses 26-27, Moses instructs the Israelite men "Only the firstling of the beast, which shall be the Lord's firstling, no man shall sanctify it, whether it be ox or sheep; it is the Lord's." Next Moses instructs the Israelite men about dedicated things: "Notwithstanding, no devoted thing, that man shall devote unto the Lord all that he hath, both of man and beast, and of the field of his possession, shall he sold or redeemed; every devoted thing is most holy unto the Lord. None devoted shall be devoted of mean, shall be redeemed, but shall be put to death."

Moses Writes the Law of Tithe

Then lastly, Moses covers the Law of Tithes. His language is not as severe as it is for dedicated things: "And all the tithe of the land, whether of the seed of the land, or of the fruit of the tree, it is the Lord. It is holy unto the Lord. And if a man will at all redeem any of his tithes, he shall add thereto the fifty party thereof. Concerning the tithe of the Lord, or of the flock, even of whosoever passeth under the rod, the tenth shall be holy unto the Lord." He shall not search whether it be good or bad, neither shall be change it: and if he change it at all, then both it and the change thereof shall be holy; it shall not be redeemed. These are the commandments, which the Lord commanded Moses for the children of Israel in Mount Sania, according to the order that the laws were given to Moses by the Lord.

I come now the summation of Leviticus, the conditions for the blessings and reflections of the Israelites. In verse 3, the Lord gives the condition by which the Israelites shall be blessed: "If ye walk in my statutes and keep my commandments and do them, then will I give grain in due season. And the land shall yield her increase, and the trees of the field shall yield their fruit" (Verse 3-4). Also, verses 14-15 cover the warning of chastisement.

Warning of Chastisement

The first chastisement is distress. In verse 16, ch. 26, he says, "I will do this unto you will even appoint over you terror, consumption and the burning fever, that shall consume the eyes, and cause sorrow of the heart, and ye shall sow your seed in vain, for enemies shall eat it."

The second chastisement is drought. "And if ye will not yet hearken unto me I will punish you seven times more for your sins, and I will break the pride of your power, and I will make your heaven as iron and your strength shall be spent in vain for your land shall not yield her increase, neither shall the trees of the field yield their fruits."

The third chastisement is beasts. "And if ye walk contrary unto me and will not hearken unto me, I will send wild beasts among you, which shall rob you of your cattle, and make you few in number and your highways shall be desolate (verses 23-25).

The fourth chastisement is distress. "And if ye will not be reformed by me, but will walk contrary unto me, then will I also walk contrary unto you, and will punish you yet for sins. And I will bring a sword upon you that shall avenge the vengeance of covenant (verses 23-25

The fifth chastisement is famine. "And if ye will not for all this hearken unto me but walk contrary unto me, then will I also-walk contrary unto you and will punish you yet seven times for your sins. And I will bring a sword upon you, that shall avenge the vengeance of my covenant" (verse 23-25).

The sixth chastisement is dispersion: "And I will bring the hand into desolation. And your enemies who swell therein shall be astonished at it. I will scatter you among the nations, and will draw out a sword after you: and your land shall be desolate, and your cities waste" (verses 32-33).

Distinguishing the Law from a Covenant and a Vow

Leviticus chapter 27 cover the "dedication of Persons and Things." Chapter 27 is not Mosiac Law, it covers regulations established by a government or other authority, which are applicable to an agreement between two or more persons to do or not to do something specified. A vow is a solemn promise, pledge, for personal commitment, a solemn promise made to deity. And the Lord spoke unto Moses, saying, "speak unto the children of Israel, and say unto them, when a man shall make a vow, the persons shall be for the Lord by valuation. And the valuation shall be of the male from twenty years old, even to sixty years old, even the valuation shall be fifty shekels of silver, after the shekel sanctuary" (verses 1-3). When a man shall sanctify his house to be holy unto the Lord, then the priest shall value it whether it be good or bad. As the priest shall value it, so shall it stand" (verses 1,2, and 14).

Only the firstling of the beasts, which should be the Lord's firstling, no man shall sanctify it: whether it be ox or sheep: it is the Lord's. notwithstanding, no devoted thing that a man shall devote unto the Lord of all the he hath, both of man and beast and of the field of his possession, shall be sold or redeemed, every devoted thing is most holy unto the Lord. None devoted shall be devoted of men, shall be redeemed, but shall be put to death."

The lastly, Moses covers the law of the tithes but his language is not as severe as it is for dedicated things. "And all the tithes of the land, whether of the seed of the land, or the fruit of the tree, are the Lord's. It is holy unto the Lord. And if a man will at all redeem any of his tithes, he shall add thereto the fifth part thereof. Concerning the tithes of the Lord, or the flock, even of whatsoever passeth under the rod, the tenth shall be holy unto the Lord."

He shall not search whether it bee good or bad, neither shall he change it, and if he changes it all, then both it and the change thereof shall be holy, it shall be redeemed. These are the commandments, which the Lord commanded Moses for the children of Israel in Mr. Sinai.

According to the order of the laws that were given to Moses by the Lord, tithes are not the most important part of God's law.

I come now to the summation of Leviticus. The Lord outlined the conditions for the blessings and the rejections of the Israelites. In chapter 27:3, the Lord fives the conditions for which the Israelites shall be blessed. Also, in verse 3 the Lord fives the conditions by which the Israelites will be rejected.

The book of Leviticus gives a clear picture of what the Lord required of the Israelites in their relationship with Him and their neighbors. The Israelites were admonished not to have business dealings with the Canaanites. The Israelites successfully completed their journey from Egypt to Canaan, but Joshua and Caleb were only two of the original multitude that lived to get to Canaan. They had followed God's command.

After reaching Canaan, the Israelites became the most prosperous nation in the World. Israel's wealth, however, caused them to trespass God's law and God eventually withdrew His arms of protection from Israel. Subsequently, Israel was dispersed to Assyria, Egypt, and Babylon. Israel has never been reunited as a nation again.

The separation of Israel as a unified nation began after the death of King Solomon (1 Kings 11:42). Solomon died in 931 BC. Solomon's son Rehoboam became the king of Judah and Jeroboam because the first king of the divided Israel.

The Northern Israelites capital city was Samaria. They had trouble with their enemies the Assyrians until they were captured and carried to Assyria by their enemies by King Tiglath Pileser in 722 BC. The invasion of Northern Israel was completed in 722 BC by King Shalmaneser V. Israel was captured because they disobeyed the Lord's command.

Nebuchadnezar, King of Babylon, began to invade, capture and carry the two tribes, which lived In Judea in 597 BC to Babylon. He completed his capture of the Judeans in 586 BC. Nebuchadnezar only chose the better class of Judeans. The poor Judeans fled to Egypt. They carried the prophet Jeremiah with them to Egypt when they fled. The Judeans were dispersed because they disobeyed the Lord's command.

The Judeans' (Jews) exile period in Babylon covers from 586 BC through 538 BC. And in 538 BC some of the Jews returned to Jerusalem; and Ezra and Nehemiah re-established the Leviticus law and the covenant for the Judeans who returned.

Again, they were not living according to the requirements of the Lord's command. So, the Lord chose Malachi to write the Jews to instruct them of the disobedience and warn them of the consequence of disobeying the Lord's commands.

God commands Malachi to write a rebuke to Judah.

Malachi means "My messenger;" Malachi was the Lord's messenger to Judea. His writing of the book of Malachi does not apply to the Gentile nation. The book of Malachi is to be studied just like a book of science. In other words you have to focus your attention only on the material before you.

The theme of Malachi if formalism. Formalism is strict adherence to, or observance of, prescribed or traditional forms.

The introduction begins with an address to Israel: "The burden of the word of the Lord to Israel." Wycliffe gives a good explanation in his commentary of the Bible as to why Malachi was writing to Israel. What Malachi had to say is based again and again upon the sovereignty of God. God is the Father, a Master, and a great King. He is the heavenly Governor. He gives covenants and commandments.

Because He is a sin-hating God and His people are careless, indifferent and have defile the temple by their lack of worship responsibilities, and because they have joined themselves in marriage to their uncircumcised neighbors, He must use punishment and judgment.

Malachi explains that the Lord made preference of Jacob over Esau. "I have loved you, saith the Lord, yet ye say in what way hast the Lord loved us? Was not Esau Jacob's brother? saith the Lord. Yet I loved Jacob and I hated Esau" (Malachi 1:1-3)

Malachi addresses the sins of restoration of the priests, who are the religious representatives for God. "A son honoreth his father and a servant his master, if then I be a father, where is mine honor? If I be a master, where is my fear? Saith the Lord of hosts unto you, o priests that despised my name. And you say, "In what way have we despised thy name? Ye offer polluted bread upon mine alter and ye say, "In what way have we polluted thee? In that ye say "the table is contemptible" (Malachi 1:6-8).

God Punishes the Priests for Violating His Commands

Malachi writes that the priests are to be disciplined by God for their disrespect and disobedience. "And now, o ye priests, this commandment is for you. If ye will not hear and if ye will not lay it to heart to give unto my name, saith the Lord of hosts, I will curse your blessings. I have cursed them already because ye do not lay it to heart" (Malachi 2:12).

Next, Malachi writes about Israel's sin against one another and against the family. "Have we not all one father: Hath not one God created us? Why do we deal treacherously every man against his brother, by profaning the covenant of our fathers."

"Judah hath dealt treacherously and an abomination is committed in Israel and in Jerusalem for Judah hath profaned the holiness of the Lord which he loved and hath married the daughter of a foreign god. The Lord will cut off the man that doeth this, the master and the scholar, out of the tabernacle of Jacob and he that offereth an offering unto the Lord of hosts."

The Lord was displeased with Israel and Judah because the priests were not teaching the people what God required of them.

Malachi is not explicitly clear with his statement about "dealing treacherously, every man against his brother." But we know that God had commanded the Israelites "to love your neighbor as thyself. But in verse eleven Malachi has clearly stated what the charges were: "For Judah hath profaned the holiness of the Lord which he loved and hath married the daughter of a foreign god."

The actions of these Israelite men that were displeasing to God were that they had put the wives of their youth out of their lives. And such actions were a breach of their marriage vows. From creation, God had decreed that man and woman should be one.

Malachi Also Wrote That the Jews Had Profaned the Holiness of the Lord

Wycliffe states that what was profaned was not the divine attribute of holiness but those who were holy because of their relation to a holy God and the daughter god. The specific sin, now mentioned, is the marriage of an Israelite to a person dedicated to worship of a heathen god. God's punishment would take the form of depriving the sinner of posterity.

When Malachi speaks of "covereth violence", he means that the Israelites would commit heinous crimes and attempt to hide these crimes from God. Some of the Israelites were having a form of religious worship but their religious worship was not in line with the teaching of the Leviticus code of law. Some of the religious worshipers were prospering materially. And the prosperity of the false worshippers caused Malachi to write, "Where is the God of Judgment?" Now Malachi states that God will sent "My messenger to prepare the way of the Lord."

Some of the Israelites and some of the Jews were doubting the existence of God because they were no receiving God's blessing as did their forefathers, Abraham, Isaac, and Jacob. Malachi told Israel that they were not keeping the Leviticus law and paying their tithes and offerings.

Will a Man Rob God?

"Even from the days of your fathers ye are gone away from mine ordinances and have not kept them. Return unto me and I will return unto you, saith the Lord of hosts. But ye said in what way shall we return? Will a man rod God: Ye have robbed me. But ye said how have we robbed thee? In tithes and offerings. Ye are cursed for ye robed me even this whole nation.

Bring all tithes into the storehouse that there may be food in mine house and test me now herewith, saith the Lord of hosts, if I will open for you the windows of heaven and pour for you a blessing that there shall not be room enough to receive it" (Malachi 3:7-10). The Israelites had robbed God by not paying their tithes and the heaven offering according to the Leviticus law.

The book of Malachi was written to the Israelites after they had returned from their captivity in Babylon. These people were the descendents of Jacob. They were associating themselves with Samaritans' daughters, which was a violation of the Mosaic covenant.

The End of the Old Testament

The book of Malachi concludes the writing of the Old Testament books. A report which is accepted by the Biblical Cannon scholars.

The Lord discontinued His relationship with Israel for approximately four hundred years after they rejected Malachi's prophecy and teaching. The Lord did not accept any prayers of sacrifices from the priests, the scribes or anyone else. Israel was left enslaved by their enemies for four hundred years.

The New Testament

For the purpose of my expose', I am compelled to begin with the gospel of Matthew, which was written to the Israelites, Matthew's writing includes Christ's genealogy, birth, early life, works, death, resurrection, and ascension Jesus was baptized by John the Baptist. Then Jesus was led up by the Spirit into the wilderness to be tested by the devil and when Jesus had fasted forty days forty nights, He was afterwards hungered. After Jesus defeated the devil in His three temptations

(Matthew 4th Chapter) and passed three strenuous tests which the devil had given Him, and the angels came and ministered to him, Jesus began his ministry.

Jesus fulfilled the prophecy, which said that "The people who sat in darkness saw a great light and to them who sat in the reign and shadow of death, Light is sprung up. From that time Jesus began to preach and to say, "repent for the kingdom is at hand" (King James Study Bible, Matthew 4:16).

Jesus called Andrew, Peter James, and John to be His followers. Then Jesus began His ministry in Galilee. Him ministry consisted of preaching the gospel, teaching, and healing all manner of diseased and sickness.

When the number of people had grown to a multitude, He went up into a mountain and called His disciples to Him and began to teach them of the beatitudes. It seems rather unique that the first beatitude Jesus taught was "blessed are the poor in spirit for theirs is the kingdom of heaven." Versus 3 throughout Chapter 5 are beatitudes. And verses 5 through 16 teach how they lead a model life. Verses 17 through 18: "Christ's relationship to the law of Moses may be thus summarized: Christ was made under the law to the Jews; cleansing it from rabbinical sophistries, enforcing it upon those who professed to obey it, but confirming the promises made to the fathers under the Mosaic covenant.

Jesus fulfilled the types of law by His holy life and sacrificial death. He bore the curse of the law that the Abrahamac covenant might avail to all who believed. He brought out by his redemptive work all who believed. He mediated by His blood the New Covenant of assurance under grace in which all believers stand, so establishing the "Law of Christ" with its precepts by the indwelling spirit.

Jesus fulfilled the law by showing that religion in its essence was different from law, and that a man who has been inwardly changed becomes a law unto himself, seeing that he is guided by the Spirit of the Lord. Jesus distinguished between the moral and the ceremonial and moral law in the two great commands of love to God and love to man.

In Acts chapter fifteen the early Gentiles were in conflict with certain men from Judea about circumcision. Paul and Barnabas left the church at Antioch and came to Jerusalem to seek council from the elders of the Jerusalem church as to whether or not the Gentile converts should be circumcised. Act chapter 15 gives the Jerusalem Church Council authoritative answer to the Gentile church at Antioch:

"And certain men who came down from Judea taught brethren and said except ye be circumcised after the manner of Moses, ye cannot be saved. And the apostles and elders came together to consider the word of the gospel and believe. And God, who knoweth the heart, bore them witness, giving them the Holy Spirit even as He did unto us. And put no difference between us and them, purifying their hearts by faith."

Now, therefore, why put God to the test, to put a yoke upon the neck of the disciples, which our fathers, nor we, were able to bear? But we believe that through the grace of the Lord Jesus Christ, we shall be saved even as they. Then all the Multitude kept silence, and listened to Paul and Barnabas declaring what miracles and wonder God had brought the Gentiles by them.

And after they held their peace, James answered saying, "men and brethren, hearken unto me. Simon hath declared how God first did visit the nations to take out of them a people for his name. And to this agree the words of the prophets as it is written.

And after this I will return to build again the tabernacle of David which is fallen down and I will build again its ruins and I will set it up. That the residue of men might seek after the Lord and all nations upon whom my name is called, saith the Lord who doeth all things. Known unto God are all his works from the beginning of the age."

Gentiles Are Not Under the Law

Wherefore, my judgment is that we trouble not them, who from among the Gentiles are turned to God, but that we write unto them that they abstain from fornication and from things strangled and from blood. For Moses of old time hath in every city that preach him being read in the synagogues every Sabbath day. And they wrote letter by them after this manner:

"The apostles and elders and brethren send greetings unto the brethren who are of the Gentiles in Antioch and Syria and Cilicia. For as much as we have heard that certain who went out from us have troubled you. Subverting your souls, saying you must be circumcised with one accord to send chosen men unto you with our beloved Barnabas and Paul. Men that have hazarded their lives for the name of the Lord Jesus Christ."

We have sent therefore Judas and Silas to lay upon you no greater burden than these necessary thing: that ye abstain form things offered to idols and form blood and from things strangled and from fornication from which, if ye keep yourselves, ye shall do tell" (Acts 15:1-29).

Acts 15 clearly explains that the Gentile Christians are not supposed to be subjected to any part of the Mosaic Law. Peter knew that the Law of Moses was yoke that the Jews could not bear. Furthermore, the authoritative letter from Jerusalem Council stated that the Gentiles should stay away from the consumption of food polluted by idols, sexual immorality, eating of strangled animals, and consumption of blood. The Jerusalem Council further stated that if the Gentiles would abstain from this practice, they would please God. For whosoever keep the whole law, and yet offend in one point, he is guilty of all (James 2:10).

We Are Now Under Grace: Jesus Fulfilled the Law

If we are no longer under the Law but under grace, are we now free to sin and disregard the Ten Commandments? The Apostle Paul writes: "By no means when we were under the Law sin was our master - the laws do not justify us or help us overcome sin. But now that we are bound to Christ - He is out master and He gives us power to do good rather than evil. For sin shall not be your master because you are not under the Law, but under grace.

So my brother, you also died to the Law through the Body of Christ. Therefore there is now no condemnation for those who are in Christ Jesus because through Christ Jesus the law of the Spirit has set me free from the law of sin and death. For what the Law was powerless to do in that it was weakened by the sinful nature, God did by sending His own son in the likeness of sinful man to be a sin offering" (Romans 8:3).

Galatians Not Under the Jewish Law

The purpose for which Paul wrote Galatians was to refute the Judaizers who taught that the Gentile believers must obey the Jewish law in order to be saved and to be called Christians, to have faith and freedom in Christ. The letter to the Galatians was written in 49 AD to churches in southern Galatia which were founded on Paul's first missionary journey.

Paul was at Antioch when he wrote the letter to the Galatians. The purpose of his letter was to advise the churches in Galatia that the grace of God had saved them from sin, and they were not subjected to the Mosaic Law. Now let us pat special attention to Paul's writing, because there are several points of interest that are worthy of our consideration.

First, we must understand that God's grace replaced the Mosaic Law. Second the key points to consider are:

1. Paul tells who he is in the introduction of the letter to Galatia.
2. Paul tells why he is writing the letter.
3. He tells why he is writing the letter to the Galatians.

Paul, an apostle, was sent from men, neither by man, but by Jesus Christ and God the Father, who raised him from the dead - and all the brethren with me, to the Churches of Galatia:

"Grace and peace to you from God our Father and out Lord Jesus who gave himself for our sins to rescue us from our present evil age, according to the will of God and our Father, to who be glory forever and ever. Amen."

In chapter 1:6-10, Paul advises the churches not to accept the preaching and teaching of the Jewish sect which had come from Jerusalem: "I am astonished that you are so quickly deserting the one called you by the grace of Christ and are turning to a different gospel - which is really no gospel at all. Evidently some people are throwing you into confusion and are trying to pervert the gospel of Christ. But even if we or an angel from heaven should preach a gospel other than the one we preached to you, let him be eternally condemned. Am I trying to win the approval of men or of God? Or am I trying to please men. Or am I trying to please men? If I were still trying to please men. I would not be a servant of Christ.

"I want you to know, brothers, that the gospel I preached is not something that man made up, I did not receive it from any man, nor was I taught it; rather, I received by revelation from Jesus Christ" (Galatians 1:11).

When Peter Came to Antioch, Paul Opposed Him to His Face

"When I saw that the Jews were not acting in line with the truth of the gospel, I said to Peter in front of them all, you are a Jew, yet you live like a Gentile and not like a Jew. How is it, then that you force the Gentiles to follow Jewish customs? We, who are Jews by birth and not Gentile sinners, know that a man is not justified by observing the Law, but by faith in Christ Jesus. So we, too, have put our faith in Christ Jesus that we may be justified by faith in Christ and not by observing the Law, because by observing the Law, no one will be justified" (Galatians 2:15-16, NTV)

"For I, through the Law, am dead to the Law, that I might live unto God. I am crucified with Christ, nevertheless I live, yet not I, but Christ liveth in me. Christ liveth in me and the life which I now live in the flesh, I live by faith of the Son of God, who loved me and gave himself for me. I do not set aside the grace of

God for if righteousness could be gained through law, Christ died in vain" (Galatians 2:15-21).

"For I, through the Law, am dead to the Law, that I might live unto God. I am crucified with Christ, nevertheless I live, yet not I, but Christ liveth in me. Christ liveth in me and the life which I now live in the flesh, I live by faith, I live by faith of the Son of God, who loved me and gave himself for me. I do not set aside the grace of God for if righteousness could be gained through law, Christ died in vain" (Galatians 2:15-21

"For as many as are works of the Law are under the curse for it is written cured is everyone that continueth not in all things which are written in the book of the Law to do, them, but that no man is justified by the Law in the sight of God; it is evident for the just shall live by faith, but the man that doeth them shall live by faith. Christ hath redeemed us for the curse of the Law; being made a curse for us, for it is written cursed is everyone through Jesus Christ, that we might receive the promise of the spirit through faith. Wherefore who then serveth the Law?"

It was added because of the transgressions till the seed should come to whom the promise was made and it was ordained by angels in the hands of a mediator. Is the law then against the promise of God? God forbid for there has been a lawgiver concluded all under sin that the promise by faith in Jesus Christ might be given to them that believe.

But before faith came, we were kept under the Law, shut up unto the faith, which should afterwards be revealed. Wherefore, the law was our schoolmaster to bring us unto Christ that we might be justified by faith. But after faith comes, we are no longer under a schoolmaster.

The Law did not supercede the Abrahamic Covenant, but it spelled out, clarified, and brought forth in detail the obedience that God demanded as a condition for blessing under the Covenant. Christ certified that He had not come to alleviate the demands that the Law made and that the prophets supported; rather, he had come to fulfill all that the law and the prophets required.

Summary

The Apostle Paul was chosen by Jesus Christ to be the minister "to the Gentiles" (Romans 15:16). Paul has presented to the Gentiles clearly that they are not required to keep the Law of Moses. Paul's teaching and writing in the book of Galatians removed all doubt from the Galatians minds. His presentation is most persuasive and convincing.

Paul's outline for the requirements for Christians were clear enough to settle the questions that the newly converted Galatians had in their minds which had been created by the Jews of Jerusalem.

CONCLUSION

By the use of biblical historical documents, I have presented to you proof that you are not required to pay tithes. Even if you were supposed to pay tithes, how greatly misused by some pastors, bishops, and elected church officials are tithes.

The Modern Church: Feed My Sheep, Not Fleece My Sheep

In the Old Testament, the tithes and offerings were designed by Levitical law to take care of the Levites - priests, singer, and tabernacle workers. In some modern - day churches, tithes and offerings are used to enrich a few in the High echelon of the church.

Furthermore, some clergy and a few leaders invest in special businesses, send their family members on special trips and vacations, enroll their children in private schools, colleges and universities at the church's expense, purchase expensive homes in elite neighborhoods, purchase expensive clothes and cars, with the proceeds paid by poor church members.

The Lord instructs the preacher/pastor to feed my sheep, not fleece my sheep. God does not want you to pay tithes and deprive your loved ones of financial support they desperately need from you. God wants you to love Him with all your heart, then allow the Holy Spirit to guide you in your giving - GIVE TO

THE CHURCH FROM YOUR HEAD AS WELL AS FROM YOUR HEART!!!

Pay yourself first by saving 15%of your income. Then spend your money wisely. The Lord owns every creature and everything in the universe. Through His grace and mercy, we are allowed to use HIS possessions. Give to the Lord as He has given to you. Let the blessings of Jesus Christ be your guide for giving and for service, as we reveal the truth about the Law and biblical tithing.

BIBLIOGRAPHY

Amplified Bible (Grand Rapids, MI; Zondervan Publishing House, 1964).

Anchor Bible Dictionary (Grand Rapids, MI; Zondervan Publishing House, 1951), Vols. 1-5.

Anchor Bible Dictionary (Grand Rapids, MI; translated by Frances E. Stewart, 1963).

Dickerson Study Bible (John A. Dickerson Publishing Company, 1973)

International Standard Bible Encyclopedia (William B. Eerdmans Publishing Company, Grand Rapids, Michigan, 1985).

Kell and Delitzch, Old and New Testament Commentary (Grand Rapids, MI; Hendrickson Publishing, 1997).

King James Study Bible (KIV) (Nashville, TN; Thomas Nelson Publisher, 1988).

Life Application Study Bible (NIV) (Wheaton, IL; Tyndale House Publishers).

Matthew Henry's Commentary on the Whole Bible (McLean, VA; MacDonald Publishing Company, reprinted 1985, 1997), Vols. 1,4,5,6.

Metzger, Bruce, The Oxford Annotated Bible (New York; Oxford University Press, 1962).

New Analytical Bible (?), pp 127-130

New International Topical Study Bible (NIV) (Grand Rapids, MI; William B. Erdmans Publisher, 1996).

Nicoll, W. Robertson, The Expositor's Bible Commentary (Grand Rapids, MI; William B. Erdmans Publisher, 1996).

Open Bible - Expanded Edition (KJV) (Nashville, TN; Thomas Nelson Publisher, 1985).

Scofield, C.I., Scofield Bible Reference (New York, Oxford University Press, 1967).

Wycliffe Bible Commentary (Chicago, IL; edited by C.F. Pfeiffer and Everette F. Harrison, Moody Press, 1962, 1962).

Summary of the sermon
"The Biblical Beginning and Ending of Tithes"

Tithe was free - will offering, which a man gave to God for an expression of his love and appreciation to God for a specific blessing or blessings.

According to the biblical records, Abraham was the first man to tithe to God for a blessing (Genesis 14:17-20). Jacob made a promise to give tithe (Genesis 28:22).

However, there is no biblical record to support the fulfillment of a promise to give tithe.

Moses wrote the book of Leviticus for the guideline for the Israelites after the Lord had delivered them from slavery in Egypt. And the book of Leviticus was written to instruct Israel *what God Commanded of them to be a Holy Nation.*

The Israelites were promised by God that when they lived daily by the Mosaic code, He would bless them; and they were to give God a tenth of their product for being receptors of His generosity.

The Lord promised the Levites the tithe, which the eleven tribes were required five to be given for their support (Numbers 18:21).

In the book of Deuteronomy, Moses rehearses the Levitical law. He advises the eleven tribes of the time, manner and place they are to give their tithes when they reached Canaan (Deuteronomy 12:5-14, 14:22-26, and 26:12-15).

The Lord blessed and enabled the Israelites to victoriously conquer and inhabit Canaan after which Israel became the world's most productive nation! However, the Israelites' success caused them to worship idols. Subsequently, God stopped blessing Israel with productiveness and withdrew His protective arms from Israel. Therefore Israel became a divided nation after the death of King Solomon in the year 931 B.C. Solomon's son Rehoboam became the king of two tribes in the southern part of Israel. Judah and Jeroboam became the king of the northern part, which remained Israel.

Jeroboam, king of Israel, chose Samaria for the capital of the northern kingdom; and Rehoboam chose Jerusalem for the southern kingdom of Judea. The sin of disobedience caused Israel to be captured by King Tiglath Pileser in 722 B.C.

The next greatest prophetic writing of the Mosiac law can be found in the book of Malachi. Malachi was ordered or commanded by the Lord to teach and prophecy to the Jews who had returned to Jerusalem and Judea in 538 B.C.

Malachi began his writing with an analogy of Esau and Jacob. He writes about a son and a father. He also writes about the reverence that a servant owes to his master.

Malachi writes a rebuke of the priests for their poor and misleading services in the temple.

Malachi rebukes the Jewish men for divorcing Jewish women and marrying Samaritan women. Then Malachi writes the rebuke to the men of Judea because they were not paying tithes.

The rebuke of the Judeans for not paying tithe is conditional, but the rebukes to the priest and the Judean men are not conditional.

The book of Malachi ends the Old Testament prophecy and teaching of the Mosaic law.

The next time we read about the Mosaic law is when Jesus addresses the law issues in Matthew 5:17. "Do not think that I have come to destroy the law or the prophets. I did not come to destroy, but to fulfill."

Jesus Christ states that He is the end of the "Law". And tithing was part of the Mosiac law.

Paul the apostle was chosen by the Lord to preach the gospel of salvation to the Gentiles. In Paul's preaching, he excluded the Mosaic law, because it did not apply to the Gentiles but there were people from Judea following the apostle Paul teaching the Gentiles that they had to be circumcised and follow the teaching of the Mosaic law in order to be saved.

Paul and Barnabas appealed to the Jerusalem Church Council for direction of the matter that was causing a division among the Gentiles.

After a lengthy debate, the apostles, Peter and James, the brother of Jesus, concluded that the "Mosaic Law" did not apply to the Gentiles. The tithe was a part of the "Mosaic Law". Therefore, the tithe requirement does not apply to the modern - day church.

The apostle Paul wrote a masterpiece in which he penned the book titled Galatians. The theme of the book is "Grace vs. Law". Paul proves to everyone who reads the book of Galatians that he is a highly learned person, an extraordinary logical reasoning person and a master of the craft of writing.

Paul presents Jesus Christ as the permanent Church figure, and by the death and resurrection of Jesus Christ, he has complete authority over the churches, and because Christ is the head of the Church, the Mosaic law is null and void. Therefore, tithing is not a law of the New Testament requirement for the modern - day church according to the Scriptures.

The Afro - American churches have adversely affected the use of tithing because many of the Afro - American churches are not well versed in religious matters and some Afro - American are intimidated to the extent that they will not support matters of truth Subsequently, many preachers and pastors operate the churches similarly to the way that presidents and chief executives officers run big businesses in America.

A lot of tithe collections are spent extravagantly because the pastor and preacher does not have to consult anyone before he *spends and he is not compelled* to give a report after he has spent the *church's money.*

The principles and practices for Baptist churches by Edward T. Hiscox has been the guide for the Afro - American Baptist churches. The southern white

Christians separated themselves from the northern white over the slave issue.

Therefore, the southern white Baptist Christians did not become involved with the social or religious lives of the ex Afro - American slaves. So the Afro - American Baptists have made the "principles and practices for the Baptist churches by Edward T. Hiscox their source of authority for policy and practice for many years.

Barnabas wrote his epistle after the destruction of Jerusalem in 70 A.D., after the death of the apostle Paul.

Barnabas wrote the epistle to bring peace to the Galatians, because the Judeans were continuing to cause disruption by teaching the Mosaic law. Barnabas wrote, as did Paul, that the Gentiles were not under the law, and that God wants the Gentiles to believe in Jesus Christ and to dedicate their lives to him.

Tithing is a part of the Mosaic law; therefore tithing is excluded for the modern - day church.

THE BIBLICAL BEGINNING AND ENDING OF TITHES

Addendum An addition

I am writing an addendum on the theme "THE BIBLICAL BEGINNING AND ENDING OF TITHING" to produce more support that the Gentile Christians are not required to pay "Tithes."

My research on "Tithing" consists of the knowledge I have acquired from my reading "The Epistle of Barnabas, who was companion of the apostle Paul, the apostle who was called by Jesus Christ to be a preacher and teacher to the Gentiles." Paul supports his call by saying, "For this I am ordained a preacher, and an Apostle (I speak the truth in Christ, and lie not), a teacher of the Gentiles in faith and verity" (1 Timothy 2:7).

The early Christians saw Jesus as the fulfillment of the Abrahamic promise. "Paul preached the gospel to the Gentiles; but the Jews rejected his preaching of the gospel. They continued to believe and practice Judaism."

1

Reverend Eugene McKinley Wilson Sr.

The Epistle of Barnabas

The Epistle of Barnabas was written by Barnabas after the destruction of Jerusalem in 70 A.D. I learned from the Epistle of Barnabas that the preaching of Judaism was still disturbing the peace of the early Christians in this decade.

Barnabas, who was companion of the apostle Paul, wrote the epistle to strengthen the faith of the early Christians, to bring peace, and to give assurance to them. Barnabas also wrote to perfect the early Christians knowledge about "The Mosaic Law."

Barnabas states in his writing, as did Paul, that "The Mosaic Law" does not apply to the Gentile Christians. He also admonishes the Christians that "The World is in an evil plight. Be watchful." This sentence may be suggested to the Christians of today. The Jews misread the law to the Christians, and the book of Malachi is misread to you today.

Barnabas concluded with the statement "God wants us to believe in Jesus Christ and to dedicate our lives to Him by abstaining from every form of injustice and practice charity.

In the works of the ancient Christian Writers, the ancient church fathers state that the "Twelve Apostles wrote to the Gentile believers on what was required of them to be Christians, and the requirements for daily living. The apostles were teaching the sayings which the Lord had given to the twelve. These teachings were the epitome of Christian morality and they were suited for pagan candidates for baptism.

Part of the apostles' teaching the Gentiles was the way of life, the way of death, and how they were to practice Christianity. They also told the Christians what their virtues were to be and what vices were to be shunned.

The twelve apostles did not include as requirements to become Christians, "The Mosaic Law" or any part of the Old Testament.

Polycarp (70), one of the ancient church fathers, wrote a letter to the Philippians instructing the Church that "They had been saved by faith in Jesus Christ." Therefore the Law does not apply to them.

St. Irenaues, and ancient church father, who was Polycarp's outstanding student, wrote. 'We have no need of The Law, because we can speak with the Father face to face."

Christ is our "New Law"

St, Ireanues wrote the Lord responded when He was asked "What was the first Command?" Thou shalt love the Lord thy God with thy whole heart and with thy whole strength; and the like to it. Thou shalt love thy neighbor as thyself. On these two Commandments, dependeth the whole law and the Prophets" (Matt. 22: 37-40).

There is not any reference or statement in the Gospels that tells us to pay tithes. Upon receiving Jesus Christ as our Savior, everything we own becomes dedicated to Jesus.

James Hasting supports the position that Christ was the "Fulfillment of the Law and the Prophets." (Matt. 5:17).

Emperor Charlemagne (Charles the Great) used his authority to institute tithing for the support of "the bishops and the parish clergy." He committed the act of tithing on the basis of his being a ruling monarch not on any biblical basis.

King Louis XVI of France called the National Assembly August 4, 1789, and abolished the Law which forced the French people to pay tithe to the bishops and the parish clergy. Tithing was abolished in England in 1830, because tithing was too much of a burden on the poor people.

My Research of the Old Testament

My research of the Old Testament states that according to the requirement of the Mosaic Law, one tithe was donated once a year for the purpose of completely supporting the Levites for the upkeep of the tabernacle, for their needs, their cares and their wants. The third year tithes were collected for the Israelite widows and the orphans.

Tithing, however, is not a New Testament requirement. Jesus Christ fulfilled the Mosaic law and the prophets. Therefore, the New Testament Church is to be financed by free - will offerings. Every Christian must give under the direction of the Holy Spirit. Spiritual gifts differ in the body of Christ, but all

Christians have the Spiritual Gift of giving freely for the cause of Christ.

My extensive sermon on the theme: "THE BIBLICAL BEGINNING AND ENDING OF TITHES" has been exhaustively presented to you by my research of bibles, history, and theology. I have humbly written what the Lord Jesus Christ has moved me to write for His glory and honor and the betterment of the Christian Church.

Yours in the Service of Christ,

Reverend Eugene M. Wilson, Sr.

Addendum

Churches that Collect Tithes and Churches that do not Collect Tithes

The membership of the listed churches that I <u>surveyed</u> is mostly Caucasian of the middle and upper class.

The church officials of the churches I included in my collection of information about members giving tithes and the <u>Southern Baptist Denomination</u> stated that tithing was not forced on the members. Some members pay tithes and some members do not pay tithes. The tithes are used to pay for church operation, and part of the tithes is used to aid the poor and for foreign mission. Southern Baptist Foreign are the largest contributors to Protestant Foreign Mission in the world.

All monies collected in Southern Baptist Churches are handled by a special committee under the supervision of the Deacon Board. Pastors get reports before and after expenditures, but they do not oversee the day by day dispensing of the finance. They focus on the spiritual part of the Churches as much as possible; <u>sermon preparation</u>, teaching, preaching, leading the weekly prayer service, counseling, visiting the sick, and the poor are the things the pastor focuses on.

The official of the Catholic Diocese of Washington, DC stated that each Priest has a special committee to handle the finance and prepare the budget. The committee on finance furnishes the Priest reports weekly and monthly. Each member gets a financial report prepared by the finance committee quarterly. The Catholic Church is the richest church in the world, but they do not pay tithes! The Catholic Church owns and operates churches, hospitals, schools, colleges, universities, charitable organizations, and missions without making demands on the poor and welfare recipients to pay tithes.

An official of the Franciscan monastery of Washington DC stated to me that the Church does not ask for nor require anyone to give tithe. Ninety-nine percent of the Catholic Churches have a special qualified committee and to give each parishioner a financial report each year and the financial records are check by an outside auditor, yearly.

My finding for the C.M.E. Church is that a ranking pastor advised me that the C.M.E. Church has a board titled "The Discipline Board to oversee the finance C.M.E. Church and the record is audited by a CPA yearly."

The Church of Christ of Washington, DC has a leadership committee, which consists of six men that over see the churches finance, and the Church does not require the members to tithe. So stated to me by a ranking official of the Church.

The National Church of God - Afro-American require the members to pay tithes and offerings. The Church has a board to collect the monies. But

7

the Bishop is the overseer, without any accountability.

An official of the Church of the Brethren stated that the Church of the Brethren does not require the members to pay tithes.

A ranking member of the Congregational Christian Church advised me that the Congregational Christian Church does not require members to pay tithes and many members of the Church give more than a tithe. A special committee prepares the budget and oversees the spending of the money.

A ranking official of the Episcopal Church stated that the Episcopal Church does not require the members to tithe and many members give more than a tenth tithe. The members give according to his or her desire. The Church also has a special committee to oversee the collecting and the expenditures of the finance.

The Chinese Christian Church of Greater Washington, DC pastor told me that the members are not required to pay tithe and the Church has a special finance committee to collect and control the finance of the Church.

An official of the Christ Lutheran Church of Washington, DC stated that tithing is not a requirement but a guideline for the Church. The Church council prepares the Church budget, oversees the collection and directs the spending for the church's expense.

An official - the pastor of the Lutheran Church, does not require the members to pay tithes. The members give money to the Church voluntarily. Each member gives according to his or her propensity; oftentimes the members give more than a tenth. Money is controlled by a special board in the Lutheran Church, and if the board spends over $10,000 that is not included in the budget, the Church body has to vote to give the board authority for the extra expenditure. The financial record is audited yearly by a special committee.

I had an interview with an official of the Congregational Church of Washington, DC. I asked the lady official if the Congregational Church require the members to tithe? Her answer was "no, the Congregational Church does not require the members to tithe." She also stated that some members give more than a tenth of their salary. A lot of money is given for education.

I asked a member of the Capital Wesleyan Church in Washington, DC whether or not the members of the Wesleyan Church were required to pay tithe? I was told that the member were not required to pay tithes and the Church monies are controlled by a discipline board and the financial record is audited by a special auditor.

So it seems that the people who came from several generations of educated and rich or wealth do not pay tithe. The people who come from several generations educated and rich families give the larger amount to the minority colleges, universities, hospitals, and scholarships.

The author suggests that it would be noteworthy to learn how the educated rich people dispense their money. Perhaps you may be willing to copy them and such a study may be of value to you.

The people who pay the most tithes are those people who need the money. They pay tithes more than those people who do not pay tithes.

Tithes

The information I have in these pages, one through two, were gathered as the results of my experience as an apprentice journalist, a student of psychology and a student of sociology.

It really seems that some of the methods which are used by some church officials to compel the church members to pay tithes borders on mental abuse, coercion, deceit, humiliation, injustice, mental cruelty, and negligence. I request that my readers read the following book that I list for information purposes.

For you to fully appreciate the methods which are used in collecting of church tithes, it is necessary that you read Ronald M. Ennoth, <u>Churches that Abuse</u> (Zondenvan Publishing House: Grand Rapids Michigan, 1992), pages 15 through 227. The book written by Ennoth will help you to make a better decision on how to evaluate your Christian position and how to petition for ethical standing in your present Church. You cannot help yourself, the Church, nor can you glorify the Christ by leaving an unpleasant situation. The jury is still out on whether or not you should withdraw from a Church that has weathered the storm through the ages and join something that is new which has not been tried by the storm. The more you buffet the gold the brighter it shines.

If a new pastor is chosen by the hierarchy of a Church, he agrees with them to accept the Church's charter and the by-laws as they are. Then, the new pastor thinks he has gotten himself established; he begins to change the by-laws to please himself according to his personal benefits and experiences. For an example, he makes a woman a deacon and forces everyone to pay tithe, which are contrary to the writing of your charter. Doctor Walen B. Harmon has written in his book, titled Ministerial Ethics and Etiquette, copyright renewal 1978 by Nolan B. Harman, Jr. (Abingdon Press, Nashville, Tennessee) pages 9 through 193. "When a minister accepts a pastorage of a church knowing that he cannot be comfortable with the charter and afterwards attempts to change the charter or the by-laws of the church, the pastor has falsified to get into the position as the pastor of the church. He has broken his contract, and as such conduct serves as grounds for dismissal from the pastorage." Direct quotes are not used in the writing by Harmon, but it is requested that you read the book. Christians use the Phrase "he said, she said" too often. Let us join the Christian Readers Club. Then, you can say authoritatively, "I say."

Your future depends on whether or not you believe that Jesus Christ is the Son of God, whether you believe that Jesus was crucified, died, buried, and rose from the dead. Also how many persons can you convince to accept Jesus Christ as their Savior? Jesus Christ owns everything. When you dedicate yourself to the Lord, everything you possess becomes the Lord's. The Lord just allows you to take possession of your materials <u>and monies for a while</u>, then you pass everything on to someone else by the use of living trust.

Some preachers prey on the sympathetic emotion to get people to pay tithes and then misappropriate the money. The Mosaic Law of tithing was not designed to feed the homeless and the shiftless men and women. The Law of tithing did have a provision for the poor and for the widow, which belonged to the Synagogue. In order to qualify as poor in the Israelite society person <u>or</u> persons would have to have a handicap. The widows consisted of women which were married had borne children by her husband, who had since died, and her children, and were not able to take care of them. Then, the priests would give the widows an allowance. But the Law of Moses did not allow able bodied men to be around the Synagogue waiting for a free meal. The Jews had then and do now have the rule "Let every man work. No work no eat." Christ feeding the poor consisted of the people who received Him and were following Him as His disciples.

Of course, churches do not feed the homeless or the poor from the tithes treasure. To feed the poor and homeless from the tithes might affect the preachers living extravagantly, lavishly, and luxuriously. Do you think Jesus Christ would come to His church in the ghetto, park his Cadillac, Lincoln, Jaguar, Lexus, Mercedes, or Porsche and walk into His Church pass helpless men and women in a soup line at the church he pastors and be satisfied? Jesus want every preacher, teach to have the art or require the act of communication that can inspire every man to become motivated to care for himself! The Gospel will cause the discouraged man to become courageous. Jesus said that He wants men to preach the Gospel! He did not call you to preach tithing. Your poorly advised teaching of the Biblical or your greed cause you to put more emphasis on tithing than the Gospel of Salvation. Do you really care what happens to the poor or misfortunate people? How can your really love the lord, when you ignore injustices and turn your head unfair play.

Some people make references to Malachi 3:10 as though that is the only verse in the book of Malachi. People do not realize you can not take one verse from the book of Malachi; you have to read the entire book to understand what God's message to Israel is all about. Malachi's message to Israel is that God will pour out blessings to people of Israel who are obedient to His Law. Israel first could not go and pay their tithe and omit all the other parts of the Law and expect God to overwhelm them with blessing. Because that is not the way God dealt with Israel. At this juncture, please read the entire book of Malachi, three times.

Some church people make a mockery out of giving money in the church. The Lord really wants you to give money without being flashy.

Some church officials use tithes to invest in commercial businesses. Such practices is unfair because they are excluded from some forms of state and federal taxes. It is illegal for a Church official to take tithes that were given for religious purposes and use the money for profit mainly in commercial investments; such as apartment buildings, stores, buses for rental services, nurseries, day care services, and schools.

The ghetto sections of many cities have church nurseries, day care for children and adults and their charges are rather high, but the help is under paid. Quite a few of the care facilities have the pastor is name connected with the institution. He or she gets paid, but they do not work in or for the organizations. Is this a form of greed?

I shall lists the costs for cases in some of the local church places of human care for an infant from the date of birth to <u>2 years of age</u> is <u>$201.00</u> per week; the cost for child from <u>ages 2 to 5</u> years of age is <u>$165.00</u>, the cost of a child from <u>age 6</u> years to Junior High School is <u>varies</u> the cost of a child care from age 15 of age to 18 years of age <u>varies</u>.

I interviewed a family that works, they pay $164 weekly for a 4-year-old child. An unwed or a divorced woman does not have the money or the family support to give the child proper care and the support that is needed.

Churches charge the listed exorbitant fees, then expect these distressed mothers and fathers to pay tithes and give in the offerings. While the pastor of the churches receive money from a department that he or she does not do anything to help with the day to day operation; of course many of the church members do not know that the pastors are receiving the money from the nursery and the schools.

The Churches are not teaching and giving the young children the proper guidance and teaching which will make them first class citizens in a productive world that is geared to high competitiveness.

The American Southern Baptists has a program that is worth notice among the church programs that I have studied. The program establishes a relationship between the men and boys; the ladies the girls are put in situations where they can be taught how to become a well-rounded Christian lady and gentleman.

The boys are put into programs directed by men. They are taught the things which are necessary for them to know to become well rounded men who know how to treat females and how to care for their family when they get married.

The programs that I have listed are well financed by the church and special Christian donations. Church officials need to do some soul searching on how they treat the young couples. Young men and women need to be taught in their teenages that it is better for them to get married before bringing children into the world, especially because such conduct is a Biblical requirement.

The Church would be in a better position to carry out the mandates of the Lord and Savior Jesus Christ if the officials that are responsible for teaching the Church members about God's love and how to lead model Christian lives. Than they are by teaching and putting hours and hours on teaching the members about tithing. Tithing is a subject matter that is not required of the New Testament Christians. Tithing was an Old Testament Mosaic Law. Christ ended the Mosaic Law.

Some Biblical scholars choose certain verses of the Bible and key them to suit their desires. Example, skim the entire the Book of Malachi and choose Malachi 3:10. They do not say anything out the Lord's rebuke of the Priests or that the Lord hates divorce.

The writer suggests that the pastors and preachers teach and preach the Word of God. For if you preach, teach, and live the believer's life, the Lord will touch the Believers heart and give her or him the desire to give to the Church.

"Behold, his soul which is lifted up is not upright in him; but the just shall live by his faith" (Hab. 2:4).

Many of the modern day churches do not seem to understand the Lord shed his blood when He was hanging on a cross on Mount Calvary for the church! The Church is the Lord's redeeming station. The Church is not a place for people to get multi-rich, quickly using methods of earning money from businesses.

The Lord demands that the preacher and everyone in the church to convince sinners to become Christians. That is really where the reward is. The Lord is not going to reward you for getting the church to pay tithe, but your reward will be for saving souls from a burning hell.

The study of history of religion is the most expensive study in the world. The first biblical reference that is listed as a form of religion is recorded in Genesis 4:8-9.

After Cain and Abel biblical story, the form of religious worship became a silent note. The next time that there was any kind of relationship with God was the biblical history of Noah and the next interaction that the Bible records is recorded in Genesis Chapter 11 when the men began to build Babel tower. The Lord dispensed the builders of the Babel tower. And every where the men went. They created their own god. But in Genesis Chapter 12, the Lord called Abram to be His true, loyal devoted worshiper.

And because Abram was a devoted, faithful, humble, and first servant the Lord made choice for Abram to be the father of the Nations. He would use Abram to establish the true form of accepted worship.

This Biblical story of Abram sets for the foundation for our discussion of "The Temple in Jerusalem the Temple was a name chosen because the Israelites had been exposed to some Gentile worshipers who named their place of worship the Temple. But Christ announced that the peace for His followers to worship Him is named the church. Christ did not build any church buildings; he left that for his disciples to do after His departure.

Since Christ's ascension, there have been many kinds of churches and temples that have made their appearance in the name of the Lord. Some of the churches and temples are devoted to the cause of Christ and some of the churches and temples are not devoted to the cause of Christ.

The true Church or temples are the ones which do their best to live by the teachings of the New Testament and the untrue churches and temples are the ones that pretend to live by the teachings of the New Testament. But the untrue churches and temples are interested in the power, prestige and money. They sheer the sheep and the true churches and temples feed the sheep.

America has been named the melting pot by some Whites. But when you check the historical record of Christianity in America, you will find that there were not a lot of Christians that came to America in the beginning of the colonization. It seems like the persons or people who cam to what later became America for religious reasons were The Puritans in 1540 AD. And Maryland was founded by the Roman Catholics 1536 for religious freedom.

The Congregationalists church 1535; the Lutherans - 1515, the Methodists 1535, the Presbyterians - 1560; the Puritans 1540; the

Baptists 1609; the Quakers 1649; the Episcopalians 1535; the Pilgrims 1560, the Baptist 1648, and none of the churches that I have listed required the member to pay tithes. It seems like tithes are a subject that has come into existence in the churches since American has become a multi-multi-rich national.

The churches I have listed are the churches that were in America at the time the United States Constitution was written and ratified.

They are the only churches, which are guaranteed religious freedom. The United States Constitution states that "Congress shall not pass no law that is "expo facto." Congress has not made any amendments to include the Moslems, the Mormons nor any of the other cults that have come to America since the Constitution was adopted in 1777.

Many of the churches that began with the true biblical doctrine have gradually changed in the recent years. The changes are due to the new friends of theological issues, the Globalization of the churches, the teaching and practicing of situational ethics.

The conservatives believe in a rigid separation of church and state and from Roman Catholic on humanists. The liberal and evangelical believe in the liberal actions. The liberals sometimes allow personal interest and biases override theological principles.

The conservative employs the rigid interpretation of the Bible and the liberals interpret the Bible to suit their convenience. The liberals are the preachers who are spends thrifts, dress extravagantly, and buys luxurious automobiles and live in expensive houses. Subsequently they compel their church members to pay tithes.

I cannot emphasize enough that the times we live in today are times in which we need to be alert and to avoid making hasty decisions in any manner. We need to be careful about the conduct of the preacher, teacher and of all persons who help to shape our children's lives and influence us in any manner. We should bear in mind of the words spoken by Christ "for there should arise false Christ's, and false prophets, and shall show great signs and wonders; insomuch that, if it were possible, they shall deceive the very elect." (Math 24:24 King James Study Bible)

A quick test that can be used to see whether or not a person is more concerned about what you own or possess that he or she is concerned about you.

Many of the modern day church officials do not pay much attention to the status of the economy, the job market, your personal financial situation, or your saving and investment account. The preaching main emphasis is "bring all tithes into the storehouse that there may be meat in mine house, and prove me now herewith, saith the Lord of hosts, if I will not open you the windows of heaven, and pour you out a blessing, that shall not be room enough to receive it." Malachi was prophesying to the Jews; he was not prophesying to the Gentiles.

An overview of Mathew Chapter 5

There was a 400-year interval from the ending of Malachi's prophecy until the birth of Christ. But there were 29 silent years after the birth until He made His acquaintance with John the Baptist. When he was baptizing the Israelites in the chilly Jordan River, Christ was baptized by John the Baptist in the chilly Jordan River and God stamped His approval on Christ's baptism by saying "and a voice from heaving, saying, This is my beloved son in whom I am well pleased."

And forty days after Christ was baptized, He began His ministry. So we come now to one of the first one of Christ great teaching sessions. "The Sermon on the Mount: The Beatitude: Let us study the Beatitudes together. You are a brilliant person.

"An seeing the multitudes, He went up into a mountain; and when he was set, his disciples came unto Him; and he opened his mouth and taught them, saying blessed are the poor in spirit for theirs is the kingdom of heaven." Note Christ did not say blessed is the poor. (Matt 5:1)

He said "Blessed are the poor in spirit" From verse one of Chapter 5 Christ teaches the disciples He had chosen to be His followers and He ends this discourse with verse 16.

Verse seventeen of chapter five tells why Christ came and He is addressing this verse exclusively to Israel and the Jews. "Think not that I am come to destroy the law, or the prophets; I am not come to destroy, but to fulfill." (Matt 5:17)

21

Christ made this statement directly to the disciples, which he had chosen to be members of His inner circle of disciples.

Christ himself said that He came to fulfill the law and the prophets - fulfill - to satisfy, to bring to an end, finish. Christ taught His chosen disciples that the law was finished by His coming to the Earth. The Mosaic Law does not apply to the Gentiles. Tithing was a part of the Mosaic Law.

The Apostle Peter - the apostle - that the Lord gave the key to the Church to stated the law was a yoke to be put on the neck of the Gentile and James the Lord's brother supported Peter. (Acts 15:2) Gentiles are not under the law, therefore, they are not required to pay tithes.

The Lord stated "for he Paul is a chosen vessel unto me, to bear my name before the Gentiles, and kings and the Children of Israel." (Acts 9:15)

This verse Acts 9:15, establishes the fact that the Lord called Paul to be the preacher, teacher to the Gentiles. Later Paul states "where unto I am ordained a preacher, and an apostle, (I speak the truth in Christ, and lie not) a teacher of the Gentiles in faith and variety" (1 Timothy 2:7). Again Paul states "Whereunto I am appointed a preacher, and an apostle, and a teacher of the Gentiles." (2 Timothy 1:11) The above listed scriptures satisfy the fact that Paul has the approval and the authority of Christ Jesus the slain, dead, buried and resurrected Son of God to teach and preach the Gospel to the Gentiles. Paul does not have a copartner. He has the absolute authority. He does not have to take orders from anyone else!

Now, let us look at what Paul taught the Galatians, which applies to every one that believes that Jesus is our Savior. "Knowing that a man is not justified by the works of the law, but by the faith of Jesus Christ, even we have believed in Jesus Christ that we might be justified by the faith of Christ, and not by the works of the law; for by the law shall no flesh be justified." "Wherefore the law was our school master to bring us unto Christ, that we might be justified by faith."

"But after that faith is come, we are no longer under a schoolmaster." "For ye are all the children of God by faith in Christ Jesus." Galatians 2:16 and 3:24-26. King James Study Bible)

Gentile Christians, you are not under the Mosaic Law, therefore, you do not have to pay tithes.

My education, experiences, traveling, and a life time of being in churches and associating with the Christians and religious people who had enabled me to have reasonable information as to why these division in the Christian and religious communities. (1) Men do not take the interest in the Church that they should take, (2) and the men do attend Church do not study enough, (3) some men leave the responsibility of religious training to the wife and some boys will discontinue going to Church with his mother. Because sometimes mother's displaced anger and frustration may be abusive to the boys.

Now I shall come to the crux of the problem in the churches. In the early days when the Americans were building in various communities, Christians would not dare build a new community without having a church built in what they believe to be the appropriate place for the church. All the families that were considered to be respected families were required to be a church member.

The prominent families in the communities were expected to have a leadership position in the church and so was the early and mid-life style in America.

Some of the church families in American developed the idea that when a prominent church family had children and they grew up in the church that they were automatically Christians by being in the church. There was no test or confession required, just come and join the church with any proof of conversion.

Many times the boys from the privileged families saw the ministry as being a position for egotistical display for unlimited opportunities, for special powers and privileges. So the young man goes to school, college and universities and study to be an educated preacher, and he follows a chartered course to get ordained after which the preachers wife to be is chosen for him to marry and begin a family. Then the church that he pastors will raise his family.

The people receive a preacher who has not nearly accepted Jesus as his personal savior. He is afraid and ashamed to tell anyone because he does not want to loose his position as the pastor and all of the pastoral benefits he receives; therefore, the pastor will run the church's operation as a professional.

"THE TEMPLE OF GOD"

Matthew chapter twenty-one verses twelve and thirteen

Matthew was a Jew who collected tax for the Roman Government. He was despised by the loyal Jews.

Jesus called Matthew one day while he was in the office collecting roman tax. Jesus just said to Matthew, "Follow me." Matthew became a loyal follower of Jesus. And he later wrote the gospel of Matthew to prove that Jesus was and is the Christ.

In the textual setting, Jesus is the "Temple of God" in Jerusalem. Now let us note the historical setting which had occurred to the Israelites and Jews to make the text clearer.

The Jews, God's chosen people, had been separated from their homeland and lived a hundred plus years as slaves in Babylon, the world's capitol in that day. They had been taken into slavery because their religious leaders had disobeyed and broken God's Law, by practicing the religious methods of worship of the Gentiles.

The Jews remained in Babylon in slavery for several centuries until one day God heard the prayers of some of the Jews in Babylon. God touched the heart of king Artaxerxes, the ruling king. And he began to let the Jews return to their homeland. Upon returning home, the returnees began to build their beautiful walls, building, and to cultivate their fertile soils. Nehemiah stands out as one of the effective prayer. The Jews also rebuilt their temple (Nehemiah 1:13) [1]

The Lord poured His blessings on Judea. They again began an explosive population. Their growth and success attracted the attention of many foreign nations far and near. But the Jews began to violate God's Laws again to the extent that He drew His blessing of protection from around them.

So in the year 334 BC, Alexander the Great, a Grecian general and his army conquered Antioch, Jerusalem and Alexandria. These three cities were centers with the highest standards and culture, education and wealth. Alexander the great did not change the culture which the Jews had practice for a long period of time. He let their culture stay in tact. But the Jews willfully adapted Greek's sports, philosophy, culture, and language by freedom of choice. The Jews learned the Greek language as their second language.

Subsequently, Antiochus Epiphanes, a Syrian ruler, sought to force polytheism upon the Jews. The Syrian ruler's attack on the Jews caused a bloody war. The Jews won their political and religious freedom, which they maintained until they were conquered by the Romans in 63 BC. [2]

---

[1] King James Study Bible, Thomas Nelson, Inc. Nashville Tenn. (1958C chapters 1-13)

[2] Earl E. Cains - Christianity through the centuries (Academic Books - Grand Rapids, MI) pp 35-43, 1954

Likewise, the Romans did not change the culture of the Greek, which the Jews had been exposed to for three and a half centuries.

The Call of Matthew

Matthew was a Jew whose profession was a Roman tax collector. It was a profitable position. He collected the Roman tax. He also could take tax money from the Jews for his personal account. Therefore the Jews despised Matthew. One day Jesus passed by Matthew's office and said to him "Follow Me". Immediately, Matthew began to follow Jesus. And he invited Jesus to his house for supper (Matthew 9:9-10).[3]

After the death and resurrection of Jesus, Matthew wrote the gospel according to his understanding and inspiration. It is called the charm of the four Gospels. It was the most widely read Gospel of the four in the early church. The Gospel of Matthew has a profound influence in determining man's ideas about Christ. It had been styles the architect among the gospels. His finished work resembled a massive cathedral. Matthew employs the narrative from his writing. He proves his argument by his eyewitness experiences and historical presentations.

---

[3] Op cit: King James Study Bible

Exposition of Matthew 21:12-13

In this textual setting, Matthew quickly ends his writing about Jesus' triumphantly entering Jerusalem riding a donkey with a multitude of people following him singing Hosanna.

Jesus enters Jerusalem and goes directly to the "Temple of God". This was a very special occasion for Jesus because He knew that He would never come to "The Temple of God" again as the triumphant Christ; and He wanted to clean the temple of the officials who were violating the Mosaic Law.

> "And Jesus went to the temple of God and cast all them that sold and bought in the temple, and threw the tables of the money changers, and the seat of them that sold doves; and said unto them, it is written, My house shall be called the house of prayer; but ye have made it a den of thieves".

"The Temple of God" and the conduct of the official temple keepers were a very high priority for Jesus.

Jesus expresses his displeasure

Jesus was displeased with the Jewish organized religion in His day, because the Jewish religion was not pure and it was devoid of the power of God.

29

When Christ entered the temple of God, He found merchants selling doves, pigeons and lambs to the people at high prices. The doves, lambs, and pigeons, many of, which were not suitable for, sacrifice. And the buyers could not exchange the doves, lambs, or pigeons. Furthermore, the area where the pigeons, lambs, and doves were being sold was an area, which had been built for prayer. That is why Jesus cast out all that sold and bought in the temple. The Jews sold the doves, lambs and pigeons with blemishes to the Gentiles knowing that they could not be accepted as sacrificial offerings.

The Tables

The tables where foreign coinage might be changed for shekels of the sanctuary served as a source of extortion, which were controlled by the High Priest Annas' family. They dealt with the Gentiles from all parts of the World! Many of the Gentiles did not know the value of the shekels for the sanctuary; therefore, They were easy prey for the Jewish moneychangers. sanctuary

> But some of the Gentiles knew the value of the shekels for the sanctuary. Nevertheless, if they wanted to get into the sanctuary; they had to accept Annas' condition of money exchange. And the extortion which was practiced by the High Priest Annas' Family

provoked Jesus to the extent that He overthrew the tables.

Summary

Jesus Christ cleared "The Temple of God" of the merchants and moneychangers. Then he announced that "My house shall be called the house of prayer". The house of prayer in modern day terminology is named the Church.

Consequently person (s) must be rather careful as to what is sold in the Church and what is sold for the Church. Also, a person (s) must be extremely careful about how money is exchanged in the Church. Church money is exchanged everywhere! The Modern Day Church Sacrifice and Money.
The sacrifice that the Christian is required to offer to Jesus today in the Church and out of the Church is her or his body.
"I Beseech you therefore, brethren, by the mercies of God, that ye present your bodies a living sacrifice holy, acceptable unto God, which is your reasonable service" (Romans 12:1) [4]

---

[4] Op cit

And the handling and possession of Church money is a rather serious matter; a person (s) need to be an able decision-maker, honest, judicious, punctilious, reliable and unselfish.

The Modern Day Bishops, Clergy, Elders and Preachers live under a microscope. There are persons every where watching to see whether the persons who proclaim to be a Christian Church leader practice what he or she preaches. The people of today want to know do the preacher-teacher preach and teach 'Love ye one another", especially the young people.

Christ expressed His displeasure at the people who sold and bought various things in the Temple of Jerusalem. He threw over the tables of the moneychangers, as well as those who bought and sold in the temple and the temple porches. The rulers of the Jews and of the temple were using the temple for greedy material gains instead of using the temple for the house where people could pray to God and praise God.[5]

---

[5] Footnotes 1, 2, 3, & 4 Nehemiah chapters 1-13, Matthew 9:1-21, 1-46 (King James Study Bible; Thomas Nelson; Nashville, Tenn., 1985

"THE TEMPLE of GOD"

Matthew Chapter twenty-one verses 12 and 13

The Jewish temple was and is a most important part of the Jewish Culture. The Jews loved their Temple with a degree of reverence. They loved the Temple because it was the center of their Religious Worship. It was a place where they could be in the presence of God.

But in the Days of Christ, the Jewish Rabbi's, the Pharisees and the Saddisees were using the Jewish Temple for commercial purposes. They were enriching themselves by selling the many things which were needed for Temple Sacrifices and worship Services. The place Christ met, and had an encounter with the Jewish Rulers is named the Temple. But Christ named the place where His Believers (sheep) are to meet to pray, worship and to express love is named the Church (Matthew chapter 16).

Although, since the crucifixion, the burial, resurrection and the ascension of Christ; there have been many different names added to the list of places for the believers to meet for the purpose of praise and worship the risen Christ for His sacrificial offering for all believers. All Christians know that there is something unique and miraculous about the Church.

The believers in Christ were Christians in the Early Church (Acts 11:26). And despite of the problems that have confronted and disturbed the Church, Christians have continued to keep their faith in Christ Jesus, and

33

they have continued to build the places for the praise, prayer and worship The Father, The Son and The Holy Ghost.

There are several names that the place to give adoration, admiration, honor and praise to Jesus Christ, but they are for the same purpose. The kind of services that are had in the places of worship even affect the spirituality of the building which is designed for worship has an unusable affect upon the individual. I began developing an interest in the church at an early age. And the Church invigorates me.

I have visited churches in many of the States in America, and in several foreign countries such as Scotland, England, France, Belgium, and Germany. In each Country there was something that attracted my attention and aroused my curiosity.

> Due to the appropriateness of this writing I will not detail all of my church experiences; but I will characterize a couple.

I was excited at the sight of the Notre Dame Cathedral in Paris, France. And to hear the Chimes being played at sun set made the view of the building was immaculate and the music from the chimes seemed heavenly. I remember with vivid imagination the songs, which I heard, played on the Chimes of the Notre Dame Cathedral. The Songs were "Zion Stands With Hills Surrounded Dr. Thomas Hasting, 1784-1873. And A Mighty Fortress is Our God" Martin

Luther, 1483-1546. The music was so beautiful that the Cathedral seemed to have been surrounded with glory.

And The Church of England was rather immaculate, it was free from visible sports or burnishes, It seemed to have been arrayed with majestic splendor, and when the chimes were played, they were most appreciative to a Christian, The chimes played an English song "What Shall I Render to My God", Isaac Watts.

The American Church varies in several ways according to the level of education of the Christians who are members of the Church. Some of the Churches play and sing classical kind of songs, and some churches. And some churches play and sing songs, which the musicians know that will be acceptable by the members of the church. Some of the songs that the Holiness people play are similar to the songs that are played in the nightclubs; they just change the words of the songs. Music is the most controlling force in the Church.

> I was blessed a few years ago to have studied the philosophy and the psychology of music in a rather renown college and Seminary. The professor was a master of education in the field of the arts, science and divinity, and apart from his teaching as a master teacher; he used visual aids and gave demonstrations to enhance his professional ability.

The professor had previously played with some of the American Big Bands such as Benny Goodman and Jack Teagarden. The professor was a master of his field of arts, including the field of communications. When he spoke the students listened, he did not have to use any special means of discipline to bring the students under control; there were three hundred students in the professors' class. The professor commander respect with the uniqueness of his personality. He could play and direct his band to play church music and without notice he would change to playing secular music. The audience would respond to whatever mood swing the Music portrayed.

The focus of my writing on how the professor demonstrated how music can control the audience, and the mood of persons. I also learned from the professor's teaching that there are instruments for the church and there are instruments for secular music. Drums, Hammond organs and several other instrument are not designed for scared worship Music that are created by the beating of drums do not put the mind in an harmonious mood with the Lord. Drums are distractions that do not benefit the spiritual growth of the saints. Drums benefit the emotional believers, but drums do not increase the spiritual growth or increase the knowledge of the emotional believers.

Christianity has been the greatest contributor to the organizational growth of American Churches. Some church music put some member's mind in a control state. And with the power of suggestion they will do what they are directed to do by an authoritative figure, such as a pastor of their church.

So, when the pastor says give your tithe and offerings, some of the parishioners will give their tithe and offerings even if they have to borrow the money. Jesus Christ wants His sheep to be fed with the Gospel; not to be fleeced by money hungry preachers.

When the preacher stands before the people that the Lord has permitted him to be over, I humbly suggest that he call to mind the words of the Lord when he looked at the multitude "He was moved with compassion on them, because they fainted, and were scattered abroad, as sheep having no shepherd"(Matthew 9:36). Jesus wants you preachers to have compassion on His people.

It is an impossibility for a bishop, elder, minister or a preacher to live in a wealthy suburb in a quarter to one million dollar house, and drive from his house to a church in the ghetto where he serves as a pastor, and then to say to his parishioners or members that I love you with any effectiveness. Many of the young people watch the conduct and manners of the persons who is chosen to be their leader, and wonder why the preacher is so thoughtless. Some children have to knock the roaches from their beds at night and compete with the rats for their food. Yet their pastor will buy a Cadillac drive the car through the Community Park the Cadillac in a restricted parking space, with a no touch restriction. The selling price for a Cadillac is from $45,000 and above. The Lincoln, Mercedes or Jaguar sells from $50,000 and above.

The preacher has to increase the number of tithers, and demand a larger offering to afford the money that is required to lead the life style he has chosen as the pastor of a rat fested ghetto church. My writing is focused on the church. And my writing on this topic is in compliance with the will of the Lord.

A Mister Paul A. Eisenstein writes in his 2002 BUYERS PREVIEW that "Mercedes Benz" targets the general households with $125,000 annual income. Some preachers have big Mercedes for himself and a small one for his wife; so that means there really should be $200,000 annual income for the preacher's household.[1]

The Volvo 560 T5 list for $37,575;the BMW 5401 list for $57,045; 2001 Subaru list for 26,400;the 2001 Mazda MX-5 Miata list for $25,640; the smallest Jaguar list $30.000; the KIA list for $20,000,the Land Rover list for $25,000 and the Rolls-Royce list for $229.990.[2]

I wonder what would the Lord do if he were to come to the ghetto church, and find any one of these $50,000 plus automobiles parked at the front door of the church? Would He clean the church out or would He just clean the pulpit out? I believe that the Lord is sitting in Heaven on the right hand side of the Father

---

[1] Randi Payton, Publisher AFRICAN AMERICAN ON WHEELS, 585 E. Lamed St. Suite 100 Detroit, Michigan 48226, November 2001) pp 27 thru 40.

[2] Op cit (pp. 31 - 40)

weeping over his sheep whose pastor spends money for highly, costly material things.

Christianity in America has caused unrest and disunity among the Caucasian Race several times. This issue raises a question because Christ said, "Love you one another".

The first great division came in 1848, when the Northern Politicians, who were Baptist ordered the Southern Baptists to free their Slaves, They refused to free their Slaves. Consequently, the Northern Baptist became the American and the Baptist who lived in the Southern States became the Southern Baptist. And the Northern Baptist and The Southern remain divided until this day.

The Caucasian controversy in America came when the Supreme court ruled that the schools, colleges, and universities had to integrate. To avoid integration of the schools, colleges, and universities, the churches opened schools beginning from kindergarten through high school, to college and university or seminaries.

The explosion of the church owned schools and colleges made the situation for public education most disadvantageous, because public education lost money, teachers, and the support of many of the clergy persons. The church schools and colleges designed the entrance test for their education facilities to make it difficult for certain children to enter their schools and colleges.

The clergymen and women turned their interest to the Christian institutions, at which they became the head masters. They received pay, but did not work for the schools and colleges. The pastor should not be paid from the education department. He should let the money go to the staff.

The Afro-American clergy copied the Caucasian clergy, in that they also established educational facilities beginning form kindergarten through high school and college. The education department has the pastor as the Chief Executive officer. He does not perform any classroom duties. He gets paid an unknown amount in salary for the use of his name. Many of the schools receive government grants to care for the children of unwed and divorced mothers.

The preacher studies to preach in a manner that will not offend the unwed mother. Because he does not want to lose the money that the school receives for the parents, he therefore preaches a special gospel. Many preachers, than and now, have become preachers of social gospels, a gospel that came into being as a result of Horace Bushrell (1802-76), Nathaniel W. Taylor (1786-1858), and Bennett Tyler (1783-1858). Each of them was associated with Harvard College, Andover Theological Seminary, and Yale Divinity School. From the debate of Tyler, Taylor, and Busherll came a new theology that some preachers preach at the sin, but do not preach at the sinner.[3] A gospel, which does not convict the sinner of his sin.

The method of preaching "Social Gospel" enables the preacher not to offend the single unwed mother or father by telling them that the scriptures says "I let them marry" (1 Corinthians 5:9). Some preachers

---

[3] Horace Bushrell - a library of protestant through Oxford University Press (1965) pp. 3-393

believe that if they preach or teach that or other similar texts they will loose their customers in the nursery and the school. So, many preachers change the Christian Church from the house of the Lord to a partly commercial place of business. Many of the persons who do business with the schools never become attendants or members of the church, because the pastor or other preachers does not invite them.

The Pharisees, the Sadducees, and the Priest changed "The Temple of God" to a place to be used for selling and buying. Many preachers of today have changed the church to a place of schools and businesses. They also use the title, Chief Executive Officer rather than Pastor.

The Lord is going to charge a lot of men for not being responsible for their women. He created the woman for you, men, for you to love and to cherish. Women were not created for men to use and abuse. If a man loves a woman, he will not father a child by her, and than leave her to raise the child without his help. Often times I find a man who claims to be a highly devoted church person with a child or children by a woman that is not his wife, but he does not support the child or children. I think that Christ will denounce such a man when he comes before the judgement seat. Child rearing by Christians must be when two persons are in conjugal relationship.

We have seen in the textual setting how Jesus is displeased with the rulers of the temple in Jerusalem. No one had ever seen Jesus display any sign of anger or violence before. But in this situation, Jesus showed much displeasure, anger, and violence at the rulers of the temple for the unjust and unholy deeds that they were doing in the temple.

Preachers, priests, and Ministers, the Lord Jesus knows and cares about your misuse of the Church for commercial purposes. The Lord said, "My house shall be called the house of prayer" (Matthew 21:13). I pray that the Lord have mercy on you for your greedy and unholy attitudes.

After Jesus had cleaned the temple of the unjust rulers, the blind and the lame came to him in the temple, and Jesus healed them of their deformities. He gave sight to the blind and healed the lame. Jesus' actions in Matthew 21:12-16 fulfills the prophecy of Malachi 3:1, which was stated by Malachi four hundred years before the coming of Christ. "And the Lord whom ye seek, shall suddenly come in His Temple, even the messenger of the covenant, whom ye delight in behold, he shall come, saith the Lord of hosts"

These things which Jesus were a fulfillment of the prophecy. Jesus was not taking authority from any of the priests or rulers of Israel. He was just claiming his personal possessions, "my house shall be called the house of prayer". "The Temple" belongs to Jesus. The modern day church also belongs to Jesus.

The overseers of the church, whether they are called Apostles, Fathers, Clergymen, Bishops, Ministers, or Preachers are in the position to represent Jesus Christ, the risen Savior. They are spiritual advisors, preachers and teachers of the New Testament. What ever the ecclesiastical person can not substantiate by the New Testament should not be accepted.

Some of the modern day spiritual leaders are involved in too many jobs and professions that they do not pertain to spiritual calling.

We as Americans speak so freely about "separation of church and state" (E. V. Mullens - p. 88).[4] But lots of preachers often times accept or run for political offices such as City Managers, State or United States Representative or Senator. By doing so, the ecclesiastical person is mixing the church with the state or the United States. Therefore it is in violation of the divine calling, the Biblical requirements and the Constitution of the United States of America for a Pastor to accept the position of any political office. The ecclesiastical person should decide, when offered a political office, which is the most important, shepherding the sheep that the Lord has let me be over or accepting a political office. When you read verse twelve of the text, you may ask the question, were the rulers which Christ drove out of the temple using the temple for the purpose that the temple was designed for? The temple was built for the glory of the Lord.

The Christ-like spirit filled Christian does not come to the church to hear a preacher tell him how tithe he can get out of the members or to hear a political speech. They come to hear the Bible preached and taught to them with the compassionate feeling Christ displayed in Matthew chapter nine. Christians will

---

[4] E. V. Mullins, The Baptist Faith, Convention Press - Nashville, Tenn., 1935 p. 88

give money to take care all of the needs of the church under the guidance of the Holy Spirit.

SHEEP AND SHEPHERDS

In my prayers, meditation and study of the Bible and other books, I find it rather important to teach and preach so that the audience that I am blessed to have clearly understand what I am teaching or preaching. Also, I want to make sure that my precious audience does not misunderstand.

The chosen scripture that I have chosen to present today for your consideration, analyzation, and acceptance is Saint Matthew 9:36, "But when he saw the multitudes, he was moved with compassion on them, because they fainted and were scattered aboard as sheep having no shepherd."

1. What are Sheep?
2. Why are sheep chosen for this commission?
3. The results of the compassion the Lord expresses his love and concern for His followers.

For the purpose of guiding my special audience in the direction I want to go. I will use academic freedom so that we will have a meeting of the mind and that I will communicate with the people who are often time left out of our discussion.

My discussion of sheep, I find that sheep are the most unique mammal. They are indeed valuable to us. We get the finest wool and leather from sheep for clothing purpose; we also use sheepskins to manufacture the better leather. Sheep will not defend themselves, even when they are being killed. The first

Biblical reference to sheep is found in Genesis, 4:2: "and she again bare his brother Able. And Able was a keeper of sheep. And Able, he also brought the firstlings of his flock and of the fat thereof. And the Lord had respect unto Able and to his offerings."

This also is the first Biblical reference to a man offering sacrifice to God. Why does God want man or woman to offer Him sacrifice? He is God, He created everything and He owns everything. The skies is God's, the earth is God's; The oceans, the rivers, the creeks, the springs, the wells, and all the living creatures belong to God. Why does God want man to offer a sacrifice to Him? God wants man to offer a sacrifice to Him, to express his love and his appreciation. This is exactly what Abel did! And that is why God accepted Abel's offering.

The result of Abel's sacrifice being accepted caused God to be pleased. When a person or a people please God, the devil becomes angered. The next Biblical reference concerning sheep is found in Genesis 12:16. The Bible states that "Abram had sheep". The next reference of sheep is found in Genesis 20:14; when Abimelech interacts with Abraham. The writer wants you to read the listed scriptures in its entirety. The next Biblical reference to sheep is found in Genesis 29. Jacob interacted with the men of Haran and Rachel at the well. Note it took seven Haran men to roll the stone from the well, but Jacob rolled the stone from the well for Rachel by himself. Jacob must have been strong or excited over the beautiful lady. The sheep was an important commodity to the life of the Israelites. Some of the most important historical happenings were centered on the use of the Israelites. Some of the most important historical happenings were centered on the use of sheep. The Lord instructed Israel by His minister Moses to advice the head of each house bold to select a lamb -slaughter the lamb; paint the door post on each side of the door with the lamb's blood. The blood of the lamb, which was painted on the post, was for a symbol stating that an Israelite family lived in that house. The Israelites were God's chosen people, because God blessed their father Abraham for his faithfulness, his obedience and his love for God.

The necessity for food caused the Israelites to come to Egypt. They became so prosperous that the Egyptian ruler became fearful of loosing their power for being great rulers. Subsequently, the Egyptians enslaved the Israelites. So they prayed to God. Now Moses is referring to the Israelite's prayers in an unusual manner. Now God is delivering Israel. God is in the process of giving Israel their kingdom.

The Egyptian rulers would not give Israel until the Lord allowed the death angle to kill the first born in every Egyptian's home. The death of the Egyptians softened the heart of the Pharaoh. Than he let the Israelites start their journey. This was the first time a slain lamb was used to symbolize freedom for Israel (Read Exodus chapters 1 through 15). The sheep became a very crucial part of the Israelites dedicational services. Perhaps the most outstanding Biblical story in the Old Testament history, is the story of the shepherd lad named David. David portrayed the story of a shepherd in such a poetic picturesque way. David had a life in which his father mostly rejected him. His father, Jesse, had given him a job, which did not required any specialized skills to become an apprentice shepherd. It was an on the job training course. If you learned the job well you will survive, and if you did not learn it well you would probably die of snake bite, attack from wolves, bear or lion. David, by the guidance of God, became the greatest shepherd Israel has ever known.

The Lord sent the prophet Samuel to the house of Jesse -the Bethelehemite to anoint one of his sons to be the next king of Israel. The people chose Saul, the first king of Israel, and this time the Lord is making the choice of the king for Israel.

Jesse gathered his sons from whom he thought the king of Israel should be chosen from. The thought he had trained and groomed them for the kingship, but the Lord knew that Jesse had made the incorrect choice.

Jesse began to parade his sons before Samuel. Eleabh, the oldest came before Samuel first. The Lord told Samuel" look not on his countenance, or on the height of his statue; because I have refused him; for the Lord seeth not as man seeth; for man looketh on the outward appearance, but the Lord lookest on the heart" (1 Samuel 16:7).

After Samuel had rejected seven of Jesse sons, he asked for the youngest son who was tending the sheep. David entered the house and the lord commanded Samuel to anoint David with the special oil. Then the Holy Spirit came upon David. The coming of the Holy Spirit upon David showed the Lord's approval of

David as the coming king of Israel. (Read 1 Samuel chapters 1 through 18)

David had learned how to care for and to protect his sheep. He had defended the sheep from attack of a lion and a bear. He won the battle without receiving any injury. After his anointing he went to fight a battle that had Israel almost defeated. Israel's entire army was afraid of Goliath. David engaged the Philistine giant in a battle and stunned him with the first stone he threw. David knew how the Lord had given him the knowledge and strength to care for his father's sheep, and he was assured that the Lord would give him the victory in the battle against the giant Goliath. David killed Goliath and became Israel's hero. (Read 1 Samuel chapter 17)

After David ascended the throne of Israel King he portrayed the Lord as his shepherd. David knew that a shepherd had to be a person who was totally responsible for the care of the sheep day and night. The sheep could not be left alone for a short period of time.

Sheep are the world's most unusual animals. They are devoid of the ability to take care of themselves. Sheep are defenseless animals.

David knew he had to walk in front of the sheep to keep the path clear of anything that might harm them. He would lead the sheep to places to drink water where the water was still. Sheep are so timid that they can not drink from a running water stream, and sheep would have to be put in a place where the shepherd could watch them the entire night while they slept. Because a lamb would not make any noise or offer any resistance when a bear came to kill it, lambs are defenseless.

David did not include the complete description of caring for sheep. But according to the history of animal, sheep had to be sheared in certain time of the year to keep from becoming over heated by their heavy coats of wool. A shepherd must care for his sheep. The Lord had proven to David that he was His shepherd because the Lord had delivered him from death several times. Just imagine a man of medium taking a lamb from the claws of a bear and a lion without injuring and killing the bear or the lion, and without receiving any injuries.

In my study of biology, I learned that a bear is among the fiercest animals with a high standard of durability. A bear has a two-chamber heart, and this enables the bear to run for a long time at a high rate of speed. Some bears can run at a speed of sixty miles per hour for a period of time. A lion is very strong and a master of the art of fighting. A lion knows how to kill a huge elephant. Yet the Lord gave David the knowledge and skills to kill a bear and a lion without any weapon. The Lord had also delivered David from King Saul and his army when they were trying to kill David after he became a hero; Note what David wrote about the Lord being his shepherd. David expresses his experience and knowledge that he had acquired as a shepherd. David is saying emphatically that "the Lord is my Shepherd, I shall not want. He maketh me to lie down in the green pastures; he leadeth me beside the still waters. He restoreth my soul; he leadeth me in the path of righteousness for his name sake" (psalm 23:1-3, King James study Bible).

David sees the Lord as being more protective of him than he was for his father's sheep. This is the first time that a person referred to the Lord as his shepherd. If the Lord is the shepherd, David is the lamb. David displayed a lamb like lamb like description towards the Lord all of his life and the Lord protected David from physical harm. He was in many hot battles, but his shepherd, the Lord, kept David.

The outstanding scholarly prophet Isaiah wrote about the Lord coming and ruling his people as a shepherd, "Behold the Lord God will come with a strong hand, and his reward with Him, and His work before Him."

"He shall feed His flock like a shepherd; He shall gather the lambs with his arms and carry them in his bosom, and gently lead those that are with young." (Isaiah 40: 10-11).

These verses are a clear statement that the Lord was coming to care for His people like a shepherd cares for his sheep. Isaiah writes that "the Lord will come with a strong hand, and His arm shall rule for him." The Lord has all power, therefore he can protect his lambs. The Lord will not shear his lamb and leave to be harmed by the cold weather. He is a true shepherd. The great prophet Isaiah portrayed his erudite poetical skills in verses 12 through 31, writing about "the majesty of the Lord." Your assignment is to read it. My precious ones, I love you.

Jesus came to the world years after Isaiah had prophesied about His coming. Jesus made the announcement that Isaiah had written about in the synagogue of Nazareth (Luke 4:18-19). I now cone to the book of Matthew, which presents Jesus, as the King of the Israelites who the prophets had said in their writings would come. Israel was looking for Christ.

I come to the textural setting for the main theme of the sheep and shepherd, the theme is interchangeable. It is not proper to take one or two verses from a chapter and expound on them. Let us therefore look at Matthew chapter nine, but the focus is on verses thirty-six and thirty- seven. "They fainted, and were scattered abroad, as sheep having no shepherd." In this setting multitudes of people have been attracted to Jesus. Jesus helped so many people with whatever their needs were.

In the beginning of chapter nine Matthew states that Jesus healed a paralyzed man who was brought to Him on a bed. Next, Jesus calls Matthew, the writer of this book. He was a Roman tax collector who was despised by the Israelites because of his unfair practices as a Roman tax collector. Next Jesus questioned the disciples of John about why the disciples did not fast. Jesus took the time to give john's disciples a mild answer. Next a ruler came to Jesus and stated to Jesus that his daughter was dead, and asked Jesus to come and lay His hand upon her dead body that she might live again. While enroute to the ruler's house a diseased woman touched the hem of His garment and was healed; than Jesus proceeded to the ruler's house, took the dead girl by the hand and she arouse. Jesus did not say anything to the maid; he just held. Next Jesus touched the eyes of two blind men and they received their sight. We know that Jesus was not doing these miraculous performances to attract attention; because He instructed the blind man that "see that no man know it." The next miracle that Jesus performed was to heal the dumb man of his disability and to drive the devil out of the dumb man's life. Can you imagine being dumb and possessed with the devil? Just being dumb is a physical and mental disaster! Dumb: (1) lacking intelligence or good judgement, stupid. (2) lacking the power of speech. We have to take definition number two because Matthew writes, "the dumb speaks". Can you imagine how joyous the dumb man became when he was able to speak! The Pharisees immediately brought charges against Jesus. Jesus did not allow the Pharisees caustic criticism after His doing His job.

Now Jesus looks at the multitude, and Matthew writes; "But when He saw the multitudes, He was moved with compassion on them, because they fainted and were scattered abroad, as sheep having no shepherd." (Matthew 9:36). We notice that there are certain things that are rather peculiar in this textual setting, and they; Jesus did not speak anything that even seemed critical of the recipients of His miraculous healing. Jesus did not expect or receive anything in return for His good deeds, and Jesus gave God the glory for His divine power to heal and to raise the dead. All the situations that Jesus had previously encountered did not affect Him, as did looking upon the multitude of Israelites. Let us again take note of the things that Jesus had done in Matthew chapter nine:

(1) Jesus had healed a paralyzed man.

(2) He called Matthew, a Jew, a Roman tax collector.

(3) While enroute to the ruler's house a diseased woman had been healed who had the issue of blood that the doctors could not heal her. The blood continued to flow freely when it wanted to flow.

(4) He had raised the ruler's maid from the dead.

(5) Jesus gave two blind men their sight. Can you imagine how difficult it is to be blind? Close your precious eyes for three minutes do you see what it means to be blinded day by day and night by night?

(6) And lastly, Jesus cast the devil out of a dumb man and he spoke. Matthew did not record what the dumb man said, because Matthew's interest was on the work of Jesus only.

Jesus showed more concern about the multitude and their status than He did about anything He had done before He looked at the multitude.

In this setting Jesus is showing a shepherd's concern. He is touched! A true shepherd loves his sheep. "He was moved with compassion on them." "With compassion", a feeling of deep sympathy and sorrow for someone struck by misfortune, accompanied by the desired to alleviate the suffering. This was what Jesus felt for the multitude, not the difference was: Jesus compassionate feeling was divine. Jesus could not alleviate the condition of the multitude because his work had been predestined. The multitude was also feeling weak and exhausted. Jesus wanted to help the multitude, He did not want to fleece the sheep. He wanted to supply their needs. Jesus stated that "He is the good shepherd."

I am sure Jesus often times grieved to the point of sorrow and tears the way that many of His sheep are treated today in some of the churches. There are so many persons who claim to be shepherds that fleece the innocent lambs, which belong to Jesus in the wrong season and in the wrong way. The false shepherd leaves the fleeced sheep to suffer from the exposure to cold and die for the want for food.

The false shepherds in the Christian world of today appoint and title themselves as Ministers, Evangelists, Bishops, Preachers, Pastors, Prophets, Prophetesses, etc. They spend countless hours devising and planning for schemes to fleece the Lord's sheep, whom He hung on a cross, was pierced in the side, blood ran down his side. He suffered until He died. He was buried in the tomb of Joseph of Arimathea and after three days, Jesus rose from His sleep. Now the false shepherds are fleecing the Lord's sheep. Their methods are many, so I shall only list a few. When the previous named do not teach the whole council of God, the sheep are left for the wolves to catch and devour. Some of the ecclesiastical persons do not teach the young innocent Christian persons that the Lord requires them to be married before bringing innocent, helpless babies into the world. Then, many churches charge the young mothers large amounts of money for infant and childcare. Some young mothers earn rather low salaries and are required to pay tithes to the church of their membership even before they take care of their necessities. They are so intimidated that they are afraid not to pay tithes, even if it causes them not to buy some bare necessities.

Some of the matured persons who live on fixed income are coerced and embarrassed to the extent that they pay tithe which results in financial hurt. Every spiritual minded individual had the responsibility to see that matters in a church are conducted in a manner that is pleasing to the Lord. Jesus Christ, our Lord had compassion on the multitude, because Christ's heart was filled with love. Jesus wants to prove to sinners that we are His disciples by showing love for one another regardless of race. Jesus Christ is our shepherd and we are His sheep.

We are surrounded by many Preachers and teachers that deal with the mind of the Lord's sheep in such a way that they leave the assemblies confused and disillusioned. They have mastered the art of persuasion, rhetoric and trickery to the extent that if they are to give some persons in their audience a glass of hot water, the members would think the water is cold if the speaker were to say that it is cold water. We have to continuously ask the Lord for guidance.

Some Preachers will use many methods to collect tithes. The members will give anxiously their money. Some even give out of destitution, thinking they are making the sacrificial contribution for spiritual purpose. Later, the member learns that the preacher has spent on investment, the tithes for personal reasons, or commercial entrepreneur, or explored some grandiose idea he wished to expand. If his dream becomes a financial gain, he will enrich himself, his kinfolk, and his friends. If the Preacher fails in his entrepreneur exploration he will either say, "all of us make mistakes" or put the blame on some defenseless person. If the Lord called the Preacher, he will follow the direction, which the Lord has given in the New Testament. When the Lord appoints a pastor he will be faithful to his parishioners.

A God-called pastor will nor desert his sheep to be on a large company's board of directors, college or universities. He can always find someone else to recommend. While the shepherd is away, the wolf will get among the sheep, especially when an untrained Clergy person is left to take the position of the shepherd. Some Christian organizations have become too scrutinized. The Preacher should devote himself to his job, and let the world run their job. The sheep need the compassion of a gentle shepherd.

Roger Williams, a Rhode Island Baptist Preacher introduced the idea in 1644 that a church should be separate from the state. Virginia adopted the article and strongly petitioned Congress to make it part of the United States of America Constitution that the church and the state would separate. Consequently, the church can not run the state and the state can not run the church, E. V. Mullins -the Baptist Faith (Southern Baptist Convention, Nashville, Tenn., 1935 - pages 89-97)

Subsequently, the church stays out of the state's business and the state must stay out of the church's business. It is clearly understood that when the church interferes with the state's affairs, there is a consequence, and when the state interferes with the church affairs there is a consequence.

I must be clearly understood that when a preacher becomes involved in a business that is controlled by the state laws spending tithe money, he is subject to tax just like any other commercial business. For example, a preacher opens a nursery, school, grocery store, or an apartment building for rent, he should be required to pay tax on the business, and pay tax on his income from the business. We know that if the preacher does not pay tax, it is not fair. The Lord demands that a preacher must be just in his dealings. Preachers should not be found guilty of fleecing the sheep or robbing the state of due tax. Stay on your job and walk upright before God and man. Otherwise, you will have trouble with the state officials and you will have trouble with the Lord also. Remember my dear preacher, "but when He saw the multitude he was moved with compassion on them, because they fainted, and were scattered abroad, as sheep having no shepherd." There are many people in the world today who have fainted and are scattered. Pastors are you moved with compassion when you see the young people burden with the cares of the world? Jesus wants them brought into the fold. Jesus does not want you to lay any such burden upon them such as "you are required to pay tithe and give in the offering to belong to this church." The Lord wants you to tell the young people about God's love, and He demands that you demonstrate God's love by your own compassionate care and teaching the gospel. They are the Lord's sheep. They need the love of God in their lives. Church officials only have to love the young people. You do not have to make any special provisions to entice the young people to join the church. You just love them. You love them and they will join the church and follow the pastor and officials' advice. If the advice is given in love without trickery or manipulation, the young sheep will stay in the fold.

It would be most helpful if every Christian or the followers of the Lord of what the Lord said to his twelve disciples on two special occasions, "The harvest is truly plenteous, but the laborers are few" (Matthew 9:37), and "By this shall all men know that ye are my disciples, if ye have love for one another" (John 13:35).

All believers have an outstanding job to do for Jesus Christ the Lord. Young sheep are the products of the previous generation. You must lead them with proper oral communications and living exemplary life styles.

REFERENCE READING

The King James Study Bible -copyright 1985 Nashville, Tenn.

- A   Genesis chapters 1-20
- B   Exodus chapters 1-15
- C   Leviticus chapters 1-27
- D   Malachi chapters 1-4
- E   Matthew chapters 1-16
- F   Acts of the Apostles chapters 1-15
- G   Galatians chapters 1-6

Reverend Eugene McKinley Wilson Sr.

You are so special that I ask that you read Galatians three times. Your reading will be more enjoyable if you read the complete book of Galatians in one setting.

SUMMARY

The church's organizational structure will determine how effective the church will be in the community. The church in the community has not kept pace with the changes that the modern technology has brought about in the society. Many of the churches continue to practice, and some of the churches continue to teach and practice the Southern Plantation philosophies and practices. Example, you are to be obedient to authority and do not question authority. Christians must be able to ask questions and challenge authorities when necessary to become thinkers.

Some churches have a patriarchal leadership and an oligarchial ruling structure. Many of the persons who are in positions of leadership do not have the training that will equip them, to deal effectively with the modern day problems. They are so concerned with the security of their position that they will only delegate a little power to a carefully selected few who are most of the members of their families or very close friends which are not qualified to perform the services that the positions demand.

In order for the church organization to meet the needs of the community, it must be able to render Christian services with care.

The following suggestive outline for a twenty-second century church is as outlined.

Reverend Eugene McKinley Wilson Sr.

I. The pastor of the church is to serve as the Christian leader, preacher, teacher and the administrator of the church. He should employ the use of other ministers who have the training, which will enable them to serve as a substitute for the pastor. And the pastor should require the ministers to make accurate reports of their work to him.

II. The deacons and deaconesses should be trained to be Christian counselors also. They should visit the homes of the absent members, the sick and shut-in members, and they should visit the members who are hospitalized. Also, the deacons and deaconesses should be a compassionate and optimistic person

III. The director of music and her or his staff should begin teaching the Sunday School children music from the age of kindergarten through high school, voice and instrument, to develop their musical ability to the fullest extent.

IV. The Sunday school (Board of Directors) should employ a Director of Special Education so he and she can assist the young boys and girls profession or vocation, which they are suited for.

V. The Sunday School Superintendent should be a person, which has a discipline in education with administrative ability. The female and male assistant superintendent should be required to have similar disciplines. It is necessary to have a female and a male assistant superintendent for identification purposes.

a. When music instructions are given on Saturdays, parents should be required to pay appropriate charges for the services.

b. The Sunday School should have trained evangelists to visit the homes of the sick young and adult people, to visit hospitals and where ever the Sunday School officials deem it necessary for them to visit.

c. The Sunday School Board of directors should employ the professional services of Medical Doctors, Psychologists, Nurses, health specialists and lawyers to teach the church membership what is appropriate according to each field.

The church is the center, the most important and the most powerful organization in the community, and I am sure the church can be the best way to improve the character, the education, and the employment status of the people by using the methods I have outlined in my writing. The Preacher or Pastor can no longer be the answer to every question. Every person must study to become rather proficient in her or his profession.

"To God be the Glory".

Reverend Eugene McKinley Wilson Sr.

Most respectfully yours in the service of Christ Jesus our Savior,

Eugene McKinley Wilson, Sr.

CHURCH ORGANIZATION CHART

Composed December 1972

PASTOR
Assistant Minister

Deacons
Deaconesses

Church Clerk
Church Body
Senior Choir
Junior Choir
Choruses
Trustees

Superintendent of Sunday School
Secretary of the Sunday School
Assistant Superintendent
Women
Men
Departmental Secretary
Sunday School Musician
Sunday School Choir Director (Men & Women)
Sunday School Choir
Sunday School Nurse
Sunday School Nursery

Director of Evangelism (Men & Women)
Evangelist (Men & Women)

Reverend Eugene McKinley Wilson Sr.

Director of Athletics (Men & Women)
Athletic board of Director
Softball Teams
Basketball Teams
Baseball Teams
Football Teams
Team Director of Finance
Team Treasurer

Church trustees are to be in charge of all monies
collected in the Sunday School Department.

PASTOR - ADMINSTRATOR

I. PERSONAL QUALIFICATIONS

1. Must like people
2. Must be sincere and have a-natural warmth.
3. Must have the ability to make a decision and to solve problems.
4. Must be careful about dress and personal grooming.

II. SPIRITUAL QUALFICATIONS

1. Must have a regeneration experience
2. Must know that he is a Christian walking with the Lord daily.
3. Must be sure that God has called him to this type of work.
4. Must have a spiritual life that is an example to the church and community.

III. EDUCATIONAL QUALIFICATIONS

1. Seven or eight years of post high school training
2. Must have training in administration.

    a. business
    b. educational

IV. PASTOR ADMINISTRATOR

1. Be sensitive to one's surroundings
2. Have curiosity
3. Have perspective
4. Have mental flexibility
5. Have an organized mind
6. Have tolerance for ambiguity
7. Have independent judgement
8. Have pride of workmanship
9. Have ability to synthesize
10. Have ability to reason and abstract

Associate Minister (s)

1. Associate Minister (s) should have at least a Bachelor of Arts degree, plus working to achieve a degree in religion. If possible, the associate's education should compliment the pastor's education.

BOARD OF DEACONS

PERSONAL QUALIFICATIONS

1. Must be a born again Christian with a positive daily Christian testimony
2. Must feel that God has called them to this type of work. (1 Timothy 3:8)

TERMS OF OFFICE

1. The Deacons shall be elected for a life term.

VACANCIES - To be filled through the procedure of election, not appointment

1. Vacancies must be filled at once.

DUTIES OF THE BOARD OF DEACONS

1. To watch over the spiritual life of the church.
2. To see that the sick and the aged are cared for.
3. To take charge of the church' fellowship funds and all monies.
4. To assist the pastor in the communion service.
5. To take responsibility for the leadership of the public prayer meetings.

6. To know and pray for the financial work of the church.
7. To show hospitality to the visitors and members.
8. To assist those who are to be baptized.
9. To attend and take active part in the prayer meeting.
10. To maintain a time of special prayer for the church.
11. To examine prospective candidates for the church.
12. To review with the pastor, the church membership roll, once a year.
    a. Each absent member must be contacted in person before any action is taken.

THE CHURCH CLERK

I. PERSONAL QUALIFICATIONS

1. Must be a born again Christian with a positive daily Christian testimony.

II. QUALIFICATIONS

1. He/she should be a person who can write well and accurately.
2. He should have good business habits.
3. He should be interested in the work.
4. He should work as unto the Lord.

III. DUTIES OF THE CHURCH CLERK

1. To keep up-to-date records of admissions and dismissals.
2. To take notes at any conferences of the Pastor and Deacons.
3. To record any notes of historical interest given in any service of the church.
4. To care for letters of dismissals promptly.
5. To keep the registers of the church membership, active or inactive.
6. To enter all reports accepted by the church.
7. To keep minutes of proceedings at all church business meetings.

8. To notify officers and delegates of their appointments, and church business.
9. To give notices of the meetings of the church.
10. To give the chairman of the standing committee a list of names of his committee.

The church clerk is required to record materials in writing accurately, honestly, and truthfully to the best of his or her ability. Neither the pastor, nor anyone else has the authority to dictate how the records are recorded. If there is an error, the correction is made when proof of the error is produced.

THE CHURCH BODY...

According to the teachings of our Lord and Savior Jesus Christ, each member of the body of the church is required by Christ to study the Bible and pray to ask the Lord what kind of work should be my assignment in the church.

DIRECTOR OF CHRISTIAN EDUCATION

I. PERSONAL QUALIFICATIONS

1. Must like people.
2. He should be sincere and have natural warmth.
3. Must be intelligent and have common sense.
4. Should be well dressed and groomed.

II. SPIRITUAL QUALIFICATIONS

1. Must know that he/she is a Christian.
2. Must be daily walking with God.
3. Must be sure that god has called him/her to this type of ministry.
4. His/her spiritual life must be an example to the church and community.

III. EDUCATIONAL QUALIFICATIONS

1. Should have seven or eight years of post high school training.
2. Should have had educational administration training.
3. Should have a good background in Bible and Technology.

IV. SALARY

1. Should be paid similar to public school teachers with similar training.
2. There may be fringe benefits such as car expenses, allotment and insurance.

V. DUTIES OF THE DIRECTOR OF CHRISTIAN EDUCATION

1. He/she is to organize and conduct a unified comprehensive program of Christian nature and training for the whole church.
2. His executive authority is delegated by constitution, job description, or directly from the Pastor and/or official board.
3. He/she furnishes information to the board of Christian education and to individuals.

BOARD OF CHRISTIAN EDUCATION - TWELVE

I. PERSONAL QUALIFICATIONS

1. Must be a born again Christian with a positive daily Christian testimony.
2. Ought to be dedicated to Christian education.
3. Ought to be spiritually matured.
4. Should have leadership ability.
5. Should have some training in Christian education.
6. Should be able to keep confidence.
7. Should be faithful, willing to work, having a generous vision, and be flexible.

II. PERFORMANCE OF THE BOARD OF CHRISTIAN EDUCATION

1. It is a planning body.
2. It evaluates the present situation.
3. It projects the needs of the church into the future in a continuing program of planning and developing towards an adequate total church program.
4. It makes plans for workers and the board makes training.

BOARD OF TRUSTEES

I. PERSONEL QUALIFICATIONS

1. Must be a born again Christian with a positive daily Christian testimony.

II. TERM

1. Until voted out of office by the church body.

III. DUTIES OF THE BOARD OF TRUSTEES

1. To assume full charge of the church's property and to be responsible for its care and maintenance, arranging for needed repairs and additions, obtain the approval of the church when these repairs and additions total more than five thousand dollars ($5,000.00)
2. To represent the church in all legal matters
3. To provide proper care for the money received from the use of the church's property (ies).
4. Sign all contracts for the church without pressure from anyone.

ABOUT THE AUTHOR

I write this brief autobiography to give my readers an introduction to what makes Eugene McKinley Wilson Sr. the person he is.

I was born the seventh and last child of parents who were from the Afro-American and American Indian ancestry. My paternal grandfather was mostly an American Indian and my paternal grandmother was mostly an African American.

So, my father had color of an African, but his physic and hair were like an American Indian. My mother's parents were African-American and my maternal grandmother was an American Indian. Therefore my mother was a mixture of American Indian and Afro-American. Her physic was predominantly American Indian. My mother was an adorable beautiful Lady. So, I am mixed with American Indian and Afro-American.

My environment has been somewhat lengthy. I was born January nine, Nineteen Hundred and Twenty-two in a Suburbia of Danville, Virginia, the City which was the Second Capitol for the Confederate States. The Suburb of Danville, Virginia that I was born in is named Camp Grove, the street name is Purdom's Ally. Camp Grove's inhabitants were one of the places that the prosperous Negroes live. My grandfather bought a house where no one could build close to his house.

The house that I was born in had three bedrooms situated on a half acre of land. My mother had a mid-wife as a health specialist whose name was Mrs. Sue

Lee. I can tell by her writing that she had some formal training.

My paternal grandparents owned the house. They gave the house to my father and mother and moved five miles northeast of Danville in Pittslyvania County to live on a fifty acre farm, that my grandfather rented from a widow named Mrs. Shelton.

My birth caused my adorable beautiful mother to become ill. The attending physician advised my mother that it would be necessary for some one else to take care of me until her health improved. As a result of my mother's illness, my parents grandparents carried me to their home in the country. I was never told how old I was when this transaction took place. But I later learned that my daddy used this opportunity to shift my older sister and brother to live with my grandparents also. My mother and father then moved to Greenfield, Massachusetts and they lived there until I became a teenager.

The first encounter I had with my parents was when I was three years, eleven months and sixteen days of age. They came from Greenfield Massachusetts to visit my grandparents and the three of us children.

My ancestry is somewhat exciting. There is not any historical documentation that my ancestors kept for historical purposes. But due to my interest in history, I have gathered a few notes.

The most of my relatives seem to have come from what was called the "Negro Middle class" people. There were on my father's side of the family preachers, deacons, teaches, hair dressers, musicians, and small business men and women.

My mother's relatives were and are somewhat prominent people. My maternal grandmother and grandfather lived across the street from the deceased mayor and his family. The Mayor's name was Epps. He was a post Civil War Mayor. Three of my mother's brothers were trained musicians. My mother's oldest was a WWI Army officer.

My mother's Aunts and Uncles were polished persons. Their children were trained in the field of education, law, and real estate.

My residence is 3101 Alabama Avenue, Southeast, Washington, District of Columbia 20020. The Lord has blessed my beautiful, charming wife, Mrs. Winifred A. Wilson and I to live in a four bedroom detached house. After y traveling in several Countries and a few Islands, I found that Washington, District of Columbia is a superb place to live.

I have traveled from Danville, Virginia across Texas; from Massachusetts to New Orleans, Louisiana, Miami, Florida and from Louisiana to Boston, Massachusetts.

I spent several weeks at a Fort Miles Standish in the mountain near Boston. Then I boarded a large ship in the Boston Harbor, Boston, Massachusetts and sailed across the Atlantic Ocean to Glasgow, Scotland. I debarked the ship in Glasgow, Scotland and traveled overland to Arundel Park, England. I remained in Arundel Park, England for several weeks.

Then I visited all of the major cities in England and sailed across the English Channel to Normandy Beach Head, France.

From Normandy Beach Head, France, I went to St. Lo France, to Paris, France, to Verdum and Reims, France.

I covered the most of the cities in Germany beginning at the Seigfield Line, to Saarbuckin, Munich, Badkrusenbach, Frankford and Fulda, Germany, just a few miles South of Berlin, Germany. And I traveled from Fulda, Germany to Paris, France, and from Paris, France across the English to London, England.

I stayed at one of the better hotels of London, England. But I took tours of the most of the Principle cities, such as Birmingham, Plymouth, Sailsbury, Barth and the White Cliffs of Dover.

I departed from London, England and returned to Fulda, Germany by the way of Paris, France. I remained at Fulda, Germany for several days. Then I went from Fulda, Germany to Paris, France, from Paris, France to Marselle, France and from Marsalle, France to Kalas Staging Areas. I remained at Kalas Staging Area for approximately forty-five days.

Then I boarded a ship at Marasalle, France to sail to the South Pacific Ocean by the way of the Panama Canal. I stopped over in Panama City for a couple of days, and stayed at the American Air Force Base out side of Panama City.'

After which I boarded the ship and set sail across the South Pacific Ocean en route to Japan. But instead of going to Japan, I debarked the ship at the city of Manila, Philippine Island. I stayed in the Philippine Islands for approximately ninety-days. While I was in the Philippines, I visited most of the note worthy cities.

I left the Philippine Island from the city Manila, the early part of November 1945. I arrived in Seattle Washington sixteen days after my departure from Manila. And I stayed at Fort Lewis Washington. And I boarded a train for Fort Braggs, North Carolina. I received an Honorable Discharge from the Army. I received five ribbons, five bronze stars and one Silver Star, and a Good Conduct Medal for my military service on December 29, 1945, I boarded a bus at Fort Braggs, North Carolina and rode it to Danville, Virginia.

I stayed in Danville, Virginia for thirty days and then I returned to Washington, DC. I went to work at the Union Station where I was employed before I went into the Military. I could not adjust to that job any more. I drove a truck for a few weeks. Then I began to look for a small business opportunity. My business interest caused me to return to Danville, Virginia.

While exploring several situations, I worked for the Dan River Mills in Danville, as a dye specialist the assistant to an aquatic engineer. I purchased property to build a restaurant and a club. I had the plans drawn for the building of business. But in the meantime, my call to the ministry became most pronounced. I resigned from everything in Danville, Virginia, and I returned to Washington, DC, to pursue an education. I have continued my pursuit until this present day.

My education efforts have been extensive and expensive. While I was in Danville, Virginia, I took courses of study at two different high schools; John M. Langston High School, and the Southside High School But I knew my opportunity to Work and attend schools were better in Washington, DC, than in Danville, Virginia.

So, I returned to Washington, DC., and enrolled at the Carver Institute to further the vocation of auto mechanic. I earned 3,000 hours of credited studies. I soon learned that there was a conflict in working as any auto mechanic and studying for to become and Ordained Baptist Minister. I discontinued working as a mechanic. I applied for a job in The Government Printing Office. I took a test with a group of fellows were high school and college graduates. I passed the test with ease and I was not a high school graduate. I was quickly called to work for the Government Printing Office. So, I anxiously went to work for the Printing Office, because my employer would allow me to work and attend school. I started to work on a job that I really did like.

I had to complete one year of Junior high school study to equip me for entrance for Cardoza High School, Washington, DC. I entered Cardoza High School the fall of 1955 and I graduated with honors June 1960. I earned six points more than I needed to graduate, so I would be prepared to study Psychology and Science.

Subsequently, I did not have to take an entrance examination to enter Howard University. I took an entrance examination because I wanted to have a idea of what I had learned. I passed the examination with a score above average. My advisor, a Doctor Howard told me in one of my counseling sessions, that it would be a waste of time for me to study Psychology unless I was going to teach Psychology. He also stated that the only thing I would learn from the study of psychology would be the terminology.

I earned 36 hours of credit at Howard University; then *I* switched to a private college. The demands of caring for my family and my job rotation prevented my meeting my class schedule and the change of hours of duties on my job changed rather often.

I earned a Bachelor Degree in Theology from a Northwestern college. I earned seventy hours of credits from the Washington Bible College. It became necessary for me to change due family and job situations. I earned 32 hours of credits at the Graduate School of the Agriculture Department, Washington, District of Columbia. I earned twelve of credits in industrial and Social Psychology form the University of Virginia. I earned forty hours of credits from the University of Maryland, College Park, Maryland. I earned a Bachelor of Arts in Biblical Studies, from the University of Biblical College and Seminary. I received a Bachelor of Arts in Biblical Studies from the American Christian College and Seminary also. I was drafted by a President of the United States of America to work for the Central Intelligence Agency. A Central Intelligence Agency Official gave me the opportunity to study at some institute of learning each semester at my expense.

I was required to take a test for a special position in the Central Intelligence Agency. So, five impartial men were chosen to administer the test for me. The qualification of the men were as follows, one was a Doctor of Education from Stafford University, California, one was Doctor of Jurisprudence, Harvard University; one had a Master of Arts Degree in

Journalism from Yale University; one had a Master Degree in Law from The University of Pennsylvania, and one held a Doctor of Psychology from Duke University in Durham, North Carolina. They totaled their scores and gave me the following rating. A Masters in Psychology, Master in Business Administration, Bachelors in Law, Bachelor in Arts, Bachelor in Philosophy, and a Bachelor in Religion. The test was administered 1969. I acquired twelve credits in Continuing Education at Howard University School of Divinity, and I did a two and half year study as an Internist Baptist Minister under the direction of a Reverend Doctor James Herrick Hall, B.S., M.S., M.Mus. M.Div. and D, Ed., Prof. Emeritus George Washington University, Washington, DC., and the University of Southern Illinois Carbondale, Illinois. My studying under the direction of Doctor Hall cornered Christianity, humanities and writing.

The question is asked, what has genuinely influenced me. And my answer to that question is that the way I was reared by my grandparents both maternal and paternal, my mother and my father also. I have had teachers, preachers, doctors and lawyers to influence me.

My moral beliefs are based on conservative principles and teaching of the Bible. A person or people should be instructed and enlightened to the Christian truths without threats. Healthy Philosophical principles should be applied to ones life, and laws that do no violate Christian nor The Constitution of The United States of America should be obeyed, if they do not violate my conscience.

My religious beliefs are based on the teachings of the New Testament, I believe in God the Father, God the Son, and God the Holy Ghost. I believe that Christianity is to be taught by Oral and written communication, by examples in one's life and by persuasion. Christianity should not be taught without intimidation or threats to ones well being.

My political beliefs are that political persons should be loyal, honest, unselfish and to love her or himself, and the people he or she represents.

My interest is to help create a better American Society by raising the standard of Christianity, education, economics and morals.

My likes are not for discussion because, I do not wish to attempt them on anyone else. And to be effective as a preacher and a teacher I have to find the good there are in the things that I dislike.

The many test that I have taken by professionals and by every day people I find that their concepts of me are similar. They rate me as having outstanding character traits. Some persons call me Mr. Perfect, and some persons say I have high Ideals. I believe that I have much room for improvement.

My hobbies are many, but the ones that I practice most of the time are books that pertain to education, writing and listening to music which have quality.

My ambitions are to make America a better place by presenting Jesus Christ in the purest form. I want to help build up the economy, improve the education of people, and earn a couple of million dollars to advance my program.

My idea of happiness is to lead a pleasant respectful life, to have a respectful family that want to accomplish the American dream, with desire to be Christians with out any pseudoidealism; and a family that take success with an attitude of gratitude. These listings are some of what my ideas of happiness are.

Reverend Eugene M. Wilson, Sr.

101 Independence Avenue, Se
Washington, Dc 20559-6000